For Bill
   my favorite pastor
and good friend for
many years
   with affection.
                Bob

1983

CATHOLICS
ON THE
CUTTING
EDGE

CATHOLICS ON THE CUTTING EDGE

Suggestions for Survival

by
Robert E. Burns

THE THOMAS MORE PRESS
Chicago, Illinois

ISBN 0-88347-151-5

Contents

(Continued)

I have not surveyed today's market for religious art. I really don't know if it's easy or difficult to find religious articles that are unembarrassingly artistic yet reasonably priced. I know of no reason that such objects can't be mass-produced if their production is careful and, most important, if the artist's original is authentic and does not attempt to tell its viewers how they should respond to it. The shoddy objects that have for the most part disappeared looked you in the eye and said, "Shame on you, you sinner!" or "Cry, dammit!" and most of us want to make our own decisions about things like that.

In addition to the possibility of carefully mass-produced religious objects, folk art or even do-it-yourself projects might supply decent articles for some homes. Not all families have the skill and/or patience to supply their own but that could be an option for many. The objects need not be intrinsically beautiful as long as they are not deliberately vulgar. Even a relatively unskilled home craftsperson, for example, would be able to fashion a simple but handsome cross from a piece of fine wood.

It is terribly important, I think, that Catholic homes have some religious images. Even the pagan Romans had their household gods and every civilization, primitive or sophisticated, has had symbols to remind them of their values.

The importance of religious symbols in homes where children are growing seems obvious.

Children especially will seek and find symbols of one kind or another and believing Catholics will want at least some of these symbols to be religious. What's more, to use a fashionable phrase, the positioning of religious articles in places of importance in a home makes a statement about the parents' values. It says to the children who live there, whether regularly or from time to time, that religion is important here. And even in homes without children, religious articles are a continual reminder that God is with us and that we are potentially members of the community of saints.

Would you believe: Humanity hanging from a cross of iron and liking it?

Less than a decade after the end of our part in the barbarous war in Vietnam we are preparing ourselves to fight other wars. When I say "we" I don't mean merely a handful of political candidates whose greed is so frenzied that they haven't the guts to draw the line and say "No" to warmaking. I mean particularly the majorities of American citizens who, if Messrs. Gallup and Harris are to be believed, would be willing for the United States to spill the blood of countless Americans in an effort to grab oil reserves that don't belong to us in the first place. Or worse because many of us, apparently, believe we might be humiliated by a backward nation.

What madness! More than 50,000 Americans were killed in Vietnam, numerous others were disabled, and our economy was so badly dislocated that, even now, we seem to be unable to break out of the inflationary cycle that our adventurism in Vietnam set in motion. And many if not most Americans are willing to begin another war.

Do any of the Americans who favor our fighting another war stop to ask themselves, "What Americans will fight and die in this proposed war?" Do they really believe that the United

States can go to war with Russia using only our present military force of mercenaries? That such a war will be fought by *them* ("After all, those blacks and Latinos and hillbillies aren't doing anything important anyway") and not by *us?*

Do those who are willing to spill blood to get oil that we could easily do without think that a war between the United States and Russia could be limited to what we call with blood-chilling flippancy "conventional weapons" and that it would not lead inevitably to nuclear exchanges?

When I wrote about war and peace some time ago and described the ghastly scenario that might take place here during a nuclear war, one good reader, with mock seriousness, thanked me for spoiling her Christmas. But I had only scratched the surface. I was writing only about those who would be fortunate enough to die in a nuclear war. Imagine nuclear weapons exploding within, say, 100 miles of your home. Electric power is discontinued. (If your electric power comes from a nuclear reactor, you may not need to read further.) The water supply is contaminated and transportation is at a standstill. Your place of employment will, of course, be closed. If you have cash on hand to buy food, you might be able to eat for a while provided you can find a store that has uncontaminated groceries and is open for business. Forget about money in the bank. What banks would be open and who would be willing to exchange goods for money backed by a government that may no longer exist?

And all the while there are the sick and the dying to be cared for and the dead to be buried, our relatives and friends among them. The streets will be littered with them. Are we really willing to accept this for oil or to avenge our "humiliation"?

Both the carpetbaggers in Washington and the phony medicine men who want to replace them cry out that we must balance the federal budget to avoid economic catastrophe, but when they propose budget cuts, the military budget is sacrosanct. Who would be silly enough to suggest that it should be enough that we are able to annihilate our enemies 50 times over rather than 100 times over?

Some politicians are shouting that the United States is not prepared to fight a war and God knows they may be right. But I haven't heard anyone asking why the more than a trillion dollars (that's a million million, folks) that we've spent on arms since we fled Vietnam hasn't brought preparedness. The answer to the problem, of course, is to throw more billions at it.

Meanwhile the moral issues in this insanity are all but ignored. Like his two great predecessors, Pope John Paul seems never to tire of pleading that we end the arms race. Recently he said: "The situation in which humanity is living today seems to include a tragic contradiction between the many fervent declarations in favor of peace and the no less real escalation in weaponry. The very existence of the arms race can even cast a suspicion of falsehood and hypocrisy on certain declarations of the desire for peaceful coexistence."

While it might be comforting to believe that his remarks are directed at Russia only, this is clearly not true. They are directed at all who are engaged in the arms race. If all the American Catholics who have been proclaiming their love and admiration for Pope John Paul would heed his words and implore their representatives to end the arms race now, what a difference it might make.

Some years ago an eloquent indictment of the arms race came from what some might consider an unlikely source:

"Every gun that is made, every warship launched, every rocket fired signifies, in the final sense, a theft from those who hunger and are not fed, those who are cold and are not clothed. This world in arms is not spending money alone. It is spending the sweat of its laborers, the genius of its scientists, the hopes of its children. . . . This is not a way of life, at all, in any true sense. Under the cloud of threatening war, it is humanity hanging from a cross of iron."

If you guessed Dwight D. Eisenhower, you guessed right.

How the media makes monsters

We are becoming increasingly a people that is manipulated by the media and, even more disconcertingly, by our own language. I do not suggest the existence of a conspiracy. Nothing of the sort. Far from being a condition forced on us by a band of willful exploiters, it is rather the result of carelessness on the part of media people and apathy among the rest of us.

Electronic journalism, of course, has increased geometrically the effect of "the message" in our lives. Marshall McLuhan tried to warn us that this was happening but the brilliant philosopher of language considered it self-contradictory to phrase his warnings in traditional, syllogistic, linear propositions. He preferred instead to pose riddles and while many were exhilarated by the challenge of cracking his codes, his constituency has never been large.

The prescience of McLuhan's insights, nevertheless, became apparent during those dreadful days when the Six O'Clock News brought the bloody debacle in Vietnam into our living rooms: for the first time in world history, millions of "non-participants," dodging sniper fire in the streets of Da Nang, trying to stay always alert for the ever-present booby traps, helping to carry torn and broken bodies to rescue helicopters. For the first time war had become a ghastly spectator sport.

All the while, in both the electronic and print media a more subtle change was taking place. In our use of the language. Television and radio has only a minute or two to tell a complicated story. No time for nuances. Newspapers and news magazines must compete. They must tell their stories to readers increasingly accustomed to the shorthand speech of the electronic reporters. And because they must also compete with media that are essentially entertainment oriented, they have less and less space among their fun and games to explicate news that often can be told accurately only one layer at a time.

So in reporting from Vietnam, for example, it became handy to describe the participants in the civil war in which we intruded ourselves as "allies" and "the enemy." Reputable newspapers did not, without enclosing the words in quotation marks, speak of "gooks," "wogs," "Charlie," or that incredible habitant of military communiques, "he." More insidious, however, was the habit we fell into of describing "the other side" as "Reds." Never mind that these "Reds" were often 14-year-old conscripts who hadn't the foggiest idea what the shooting was all about and whose only ideology was living to be 15.

But describing the Viet Cong and Vietnamese from the North as "Reds" had a certain primitive logic. They were shooting at Americans and Americans were shooting at them and, we were told, the governments they represented were Marxist. (How embarrassing it would have been to have put a group of the generals commanding the American efforts in Vietnam on the Six O'Clock News and to have asked them to explain what Marxist means.) The fallout from this practice of pasting neat and simple labels on matters that require precise and often subtle distinctions became far more serious when the news media began calling people and groups "Reds," "Marxist," and "leftist" on a world-wide basis.

Despite the fact that we have decided that it is in our national interest to ally ourselves with the "Red" Chinese in opposition to the "Red" Russians, all of these labels continue to have the connotation "enemy" for Americans. Despite the fact that we have considered it in our national interest to cooperate in varying degrees with such "Red" governments as Yugoslavia, Romania, and Poland, the news media continue to toss these terms around knowing that most of their viewers and readers receive them as dirty words.

When the funeral of the martyred Archbishop Romero in El Salvador was turned into a near riot by bombs and gunfire, the American news media considered themselves responsible by describing the sad incident as a battle between leftists and rightists with some blaming one group and some the other. When the news media who should know and tell better fail to describe the social and economic conditions, the maldistribution of wealth with a handful of powerful exploiters and their hired assassins ruthlessly suppressing all others, it is no wonder that the United States Congress that should know better chooses to send aid to any politicians who claim to oppose their "leftists."

How ironic it is then that our personal and political morality is often shaped as it is because we are unable or unwilling to define with precision the words we use. It would be comforting if we could believe that the news media would begin to act more responsibly by making it clear that most life issues are shades of gray, not black and white (red & white?). But don't count on that. Each of us will probably have to take the responsibility for making our own distinctions if we are to survive.

Our help, in any event, is in the name of the Lord

In some circles it has become fashionable during the past couple of decades to downgrade prayers of petition. Coteries of the faithful who consider themselves more enlightened than their unwashed sisters and brothers turn their noses up at the idea of asking God for favors. Prayer, they seem to be saying, should be pure. It should not be self-serving and in particular it should not be questing for material favors.

This snobbery probably began as something quite worthwhile. Prayer, for many, had become almost exclusively asking for favors. Like the nine lepers a lot of us asked and received favors and forgot to say, "Thank you." And in our concentration on asking, we were even less likely to offer the so-called pure prayers of praise to God. Most of the Mass prayers are, of course, prayers of praise but, particularly in the bad old days when we were relatively uninvolved, the Mass prayers tended to be more his than ours. It was when we needed something—a job, cure of an illness, the soothing of a family conflict, good grades on final exams—that we did our serious praying. I confess that as a small boy I would place a miniature statue of Our Lady of Grace or St. Anthony (I hadn't yet learned about St. Jude) outside a bedroom window the night before a scheduled picnic to guarantee good weather. (And, you know, it usually worked!)

No doubt, many of us gave asking prayers a disproportionate emphasis. But prayers of petition didn't deserve the scorn that was heaped on them. "Gimme prayers," as the scornful called them, were ranked only slightly higher than sins of omission in the spiritual pecking order. These critics, presumably, were embarrassed that many people were humble enough to voice their needs while praying. (Oh, how they must have shuddered at the thought that some even wrote their requests on petition slips of paper.)

The views of the critics may be good theology but they're rotten psychology. We humans just don't work the way they would like us to and that, of course, is what we are, humans not angels. It's all very well to say that God knows our needs. Sure he does. But a lot of us think it would be dumb to try to converse with God, remaining all the while coy about the problems and hopes that occupy most of our lives.

In jousting with the critics of asking prayers, I've used the past tense because I think that, for now at least, the worst is over. Some of the most articulate of these critics now demonstrate little interest in anything religious. Others, for one reason or another, seem not be exercised in the matter. But to some extent, the past continues to be prologue. Some continue to be embarrassed when they hear that many trusting persons have no hesitation in asking God to help them find a suitable wife or husband or to help them get out of overbearing debt.

Asking prayers are where praying begins. The bedtime prayers of the small child, "God bless Mom and Dad and keep us all safe through the night," are surely asking prayers. And while our praying shouldn't end with asking, asking should always be part of them.

I'm not a member of any of the prayer groups, both public and private, that have sprung up widely during the last decade but I don't think there can be much doubt that the existence of these groups is a sign of splendid vitality in the church. Some of these groups are called "charismatic" but I've found that to be a broad word that means different things in different places and I like that, too. Many of these groups, I understand, give high priority to demonstrating their faith in God by praising him, sometimes with uninhibited fervor. That, I think, is not only sound theologically but healthy psychologically. Praise the Lord!

If an outsider may be permitted, I offer two bits of advice to such prayer groups. The first is a suggestion that may already have been adopted by many of the groups. I suggest that they regularly audit the effect of their prayers in common on their personal lives. Have their prayers scoured away some of their pride and made them more humble? Or do they find themselves, like the Pharisee, looking down their noses at the unwashed outside of the group?

Have their prayers made them more patient and more charitable toward others or do they continue to laugh without qualms at the brittle joke at someone else's expense.

Finally, I suggest that prayer groups might consider a "sunset law" that would cause them to dissolve after they had prayed together for a reasonable length of time. Groups with a considerable interchange of membership might stay together fruitfully for a longer time than tight little groups. But any relatively small praying group runs the risk, I believe, of falling into spiritual incest, looking in increasingly and becoming less and less interested in the kind of outreach that prayer is intended to engender.

Praying together shouldn't always mean staying together.

Uncertainty: One thing
we can be certain of

There is a lot of truth in the old saw that we can learn more from bad situations than from good. To trot out once again the "in" phrase, a painful encounter is far more likely to be "a learning experience" than is an occasion we enjoy.

Those of us who hold religious beliefs and particularly those of us who hold religious affiliations ought to find our American confrontation with the fanatical theocrats in Iran a most valuable learning experience. The Persian ayatollahs and other "holy men" who seem to be in control in that unhappy country rule not only with the iron hand that is common to all dictators but with the absolute certainty that they are always right that is uniquely theocratic. A ruthless Josef Stalin or Anastasio Somoza isn't at all concerned with whether or not what he has said or done is right; he is concerned only with whether it will work. An Ayatollah Khomeini is convinced that what he says and does is right whether or not it works.

I am moved to make these comments because, it seems to me, an increasing number of Catholics and other Christians have begun to speak, write, and act like ayatollahs. Without so much as a "I may be mistaken but," this growing multitude is ready to pass swift and inexorable judgment on all with whom they disagree.

These mini-ayatollahs seem to be popping up everywhere, on commuter trains, on radio talk shows, in what used to be mild-mannered social groupings, even among readers of *U.S. Catholic.* (I have always found the latter to be far more reasonable and temperate than the public at large and I have every reason to believe that most *U.S. Catholic* readers are like that. I'd like to believe that those few who hurl their I-have-it-straight-from God-judgments at us are not regular readers but casuals who have picked up an occasional copy.)

Some of those who rain their infallible judgments on the heads of unfortunate dissidents offer no reasons at all for their judgments. The reasons are presumably self-evident, to the judges at least. Others have discovered, at long last, the Bible and a handy-dandy book it is for those who do a lot of judging. If you object to discussing homosexuality, there's good old Leviticus. If you've irretrievably made up your mind that frying poor people in an electric chair will reduce crime, there's "an eye for an eye, etc." And if Dan Berrigan writing about derelicts trying to keep warm in an urban winter disturbs you in the serenity of Marcos Island, what about, "the poor we shall always have with us"? (A purely emotional, unreasoning reaction to these specious judgments is a nostalgia for the days when "Catholic Bibles" were chained to lecterns and the faithful were warned against reading the Scriptures.)

A social psychologist or a religious anthropologist, perhaps, is needed to explain with precision this urge to judge others with utter finality. But an amateur guess would probably point to the uneasiness that afflicts us today in a time when so many once comforting "certainties" have come unhinged. Never mind that these certainties were never really that. Never mind that what we now look back upon as certainties were only approximations. So much of our lives was habitually unexamined that we didn't notice until the boat began to rock that a lot of things weren't fastened down.

Nonbelievers tend to think that it is believers who are most likely to hand down unequivocal judgments of the other kind I have been discussing but it should be, I think, the other way around. True believers ought to be the slowest to judge, the most ready to find justification for those whose words and actions we disagree with. Believers, ironically, ought to welcome at least the degree of uncertainty that distinguishes the human from the divine. More than that, I believe, Christians should welcome uncertainty as making it possible for us to stand humble before God.

Sydney J. Harris has wisely pointed out that "any church, no matter what its pipeline to heaven, is but a hopeful approximation of the divine order, as susceptible to weakness, error, cruelty and corruption as any other temporal agency. Even the most devout cannot claim to know how God would act; even St. Thomas admitted we can 'know' Him only by what He is not, not by what He is."

If each of us would weigh these words before taking pen in hand to write an editor, pick up a phone to call a radio station, or issue a proclamation at a barbecue, we might, just might, sound more like people and less like the God of movies.

Half a loaf is still crumbs

Every year about this time, Catholic leaders, especially Catholic educators, tend to become exercised about the second-class status of Catholic schools. Not that Catholic schools are second class. With all their faults, they seem, for the most part, to check out as well or better than American public schools. I am referring to the status of Catholic schools in the eyes of our various governmental bodies.

Time after time, efforts to help the financially hard-pressed private schools (read Catholic schools here) are slapped down by courts or civil administrators usually on the grounds that helping them would constitute a violation of the traditional separation of church and state. Actually, the latter "tradition" is a projection that has evolved over the years, fleshing out the bare bones of a precept in the U.S. Constitution that "Congress shall make no law regarding the establishment of religion." And some of the interpretations that have spun off of that precept might very well bewilder the framers of that document.

At various times and in various places, for example, school buses have been required to bypass children on their way to Catholic schools leaving them at the mercy of the elements no matter how harsh. The use of public funds to pay for standardized testing of Catholic school students at neutrally located testing centers has been proscribed as has the sharing of athletic and recreational facilities by students of public and private schools.

Recently a legislative attempt by Senator Daniel P. Moynihan of New York to provide financial aid to low and middle income families whose children attend nonpublic schools was shot down in the U.S. Senate. The demise of the Moynihan bill elicited an exasperated outburst from Archbishop John R. Roach of St. Paul-Minneapolis and the archbishop pointed the finger of blame for this in precisely the right direction. "I am tired," he said, "of taking it on the chin from public education lobbies."

"As our population declines and as school enrollments drop," Archbishop Roach said, "each child in a nonpublic school is a threat to somebody's job and to the enormous bureaucracy which supports public education."

Tough talk like this is unlikely to win for the archbishop the For He's a Jolly Good Fellow Award of the National Education Association but I think it's the kind of thing that needs saying.

The NEA and several kindred and politically muscular organizations were at one time considerably more doctrinaire than they are today. In our early history the idea of free public education for all citizens was understandably attractive to people who had fled from a Europe in which only the affluent could afford to educate their children. Free public education was an even more basic part of the American dream than was universal suffrage, the right to vote being restricted to white males for more than a century. But before long the inevitable bureaucracy grew up in and around public education and that worthy concept became more than a right. It became a principal tenet in American civil religion and those who would not bend a knee to it became suspect if not heretical.

For a while the existence of Catholic schools didn't bother the public school zealots. Their students, largely, were from ethnic immigrant families and it was just as well that their kind didn't clutter up pure American schools. But that attitude began to change as Catholics were "Americanized" and Catholic school student bodies couldn't be distinguished from those attending P.S. 101 down the street.

The civil-religion fervor of public-school bureaucrats has, of course, diminished in the second half of this century. The issues between public and nonpublic schools are now mostly pragmatic. As all educational costs increase, the competition for the financial support of the citizenry, taxes for public schools, tuition and donations for private schools, has sharpened. And the public education lobbies, though stronger than ever, are no longer winning every battle. In the words of Archbishop Roach, "they are running scared."

Although I share the archbishop's exasperation, I think it's just as well that well-intentioned but Band-aid solutions to the problem are being rejected. American Catholic schools—and for that matter American public schools—will not get their due until the funding of elementary and secondary education is radically restructured. The only reasonable answer to the problem is a voucher system with every child receiving a standardized credit to be expended at an accredited school, public or private, religious or secular, chosen by the family. Such a solution would do wonders for the quality of education in the United States if only because competition would make it impossible for inferior schools to survive.

In the past the voucher system has not been possible because of the strength of the public-school lobbies and that, probably, is still true today. But I think the time is ripe for Catholics and other believers in "private" schools to persuade the general (voting) public that the voucher system makes a lot of sense. I'm not suggesting that traditional Catholic lobbying be abandoned but I am suggesting that Catholics stop begging for crumbs from legislative tables. We should band together with those of other faiths who feel as we do and convince the American public that every child should be treated equally when we spend our money for education.

American religion:
Soul-felt or skin-deep?

Americans are probably more religious than any people in modern times. Or are they? A stranger from another planet would probably say "Yes." It's difficult to walk several blocks in any American town, small, medium, or large, without encountering a church. Our currency bears the legend, "In God We Trust" and it's a rare civil function that does not begin with prayer. An overwhelming majority of us express our belief in God and far more than half belong to a church or synagogue. And the most authoritative polls attest that nearly all Americans pray.

But there is little indication that this pervasive religiosity affects the lives and actions of Americans deeply. By their own admission, religion doesn't matter a lot to most of us. As reported by Religious News Service, a recent survey made in predominantly Catholic Boston, for example, revealed that little more than half of the church members attend services regularly and a large majority do not read the Bible, never or rarely say grace at meals, do not refer to a religious book in making important decisions, and do not tune in to religious programs on radio or television.

According to the survey, only five percent of the population of Greater Boston would turn to a member of the clergy in time of serious need or trouble. Among church members, the figure was seven percent. And only three percent said that a minister or priest had the greatest influence on their lives.

The Boston survey also puts its finger on two sore spots on the American religious body. The first is that religious observance declined in inverse proportion to the level of personal income. About one third of those making $30,000 a year or more frequented church while more than half the respondents earning $10,000 or less went regularly. Forty-one percent of the wealthiest survey category prayed while 72 percent of the poorest said they did. "The dropouts are upwardly mobile, socially and geographically, persons with college degrees and solid incomes—especially those who came of age in the '60s," one commentator on the survey remarked.

This latter conclusion may have been skewed by the fact that blacks surveyed, far more than whites, were inclined to practice their religion. Seventy-two percent of them, as opposed to 56 percent of whites, said they prayed. More than half the blacks said grace before meals and 45 percent followed religious broadcasts. Whites registered positive responses of only 14 percent and 12 percent in these two categories. And it is safe to assume that the blacks surveyed were significantly less affluent than the whites.

The second sore point is, even more, a cause for concern. The survey showed that adults aged 30 to 44 were the least religious; less than ten percent of them ever attended church regularly or read the Bible. Meanwhile a second poll, conducted by Dr. Dean Hoge of Catholic University of America, tended to confirm and explain the erosion of religious practice among young adults. Surveying Catholics only, Dr. Hoge's study reported that a majority of those who leave the church do so before the age of 25. Thirty-five percent of the young adults drop out of the church by age 20 and that figure increases to 54 percent by age 25. He said that this youthful alienation from the faith is so common throughout Christian denominations that it is almost normal statistically.

The reasons offered by the defecting young adults are interesting. Most of those polled left the church because they found it "boring and uninteresting." More than half of those under 22 said they left the church because they were rebelling against their parents' putting too much emphasis on churchgoing. Others who left include "lifestyle dropouts" who have problems with the church's moral teachings; "spiritual-need dropouts" who seek spirituality in other churches or faiths; and "anti-change dropouts" (about seven percent) who refuse to accept the post-Vatican II changes in the church.

Those who are, understandably, discouraged by the attrition among young Catholics may find hope in the recently expressed views of Archbishop William Borders of Baltimore. Interviewed by the *National Catholic Reporter,* the archbishop agreed that the age group "22 to 40 is the weakest we have in U.S. Catholicism." But, he went on to say, "I've never seen such a radical improvement in adolescents as in the last five years. I'm really confident—because these young people are beginning to recognize real values, they're different than the kids of 10 years ago."

Those who care for the present and particularly the future health of the church will find a much needed ray of hope in those words of Archbishop Borders, words that are confirmed by the testimony of others who work among adolescent Catholics. Let's pray also that this new generation of Catholics will have learned what our generations have learned imperfectly if at all, that mere church attendance and religious observance is all but meaningless if our religious beliefs do not influence every phase of our lives.

For the President's Christmas stocking: An agenda

When you read this, the American people will have chosen the man who will be their president (I almost wrote, "whom they wish to be their president") for the next four years. This man has emerged victorious from a political campaign that can be described, at best, as "messy" and, at worst, as appalling.

Closely contested political campaigns tend strongly to mediocritize the contestants and the presidential campaign of 1980 has not been an exception. Let one contender pronounce that we must spend five billion more for nuclear weapons, the other will quickly respond that we should spend ten billion. When one promises a 10 percent tax cut, his opponent will lose no time in favoring a tax cut twice as large. Neither dares to tell the electorate that they must make hard choices. Both must promise pie-in-the-sky not only to the populace as a whole but to every ethnic, religious, racial, and occupational group. To speak unpopular words to any of these is deemed far too risky when Messrs. Gallup and Harris are projecting paper-thin margins on election day.

But, mercifully, all political campaigns end eventually and, *mirabile dictu*, the presidential campaign of 1980 is over. Is it too much to ask (I do not say "expect") that now the elected or re-elected president stop acting like a candidate and begin acting like a statesman? Don't we have a right to ask our president to lead rather than follow the opinion polls? To lead not only us but all people of goodwill everywhere?

The President has not (yet?) asked for my help but I offer it freely here by suggesting an agenda for his next few years:

First priority must be given to stopping the arms race. It is immoral and insane. If it does not lead soon to a catastrophic war that will destroy not only our cities but our civilization, it will in the interim bankrupt us, our friends, and our adversaries, a bankruptcy that will leave our civilization in shreds.

It is not necessary to believe naively that the leaders of the Soviet Union are gentle and virtuous men to believe that they must be aware that a continuing arms race can lead only to the bankruptcies of both their economy and ours and to mutual and irreparable destruction of our societies.

If the gradual dismantling of our nuclear arsenals is not immediately possible (and it may not be), we must insist on a mutual freezing of them in the hope, scientifically justifiable, that our nuclear weaponry will in 5, 10, or 20 years deteriorate to the point of near uselessness.

The President of the United States must make clear to the American people that the so-called nuclear alternative is not an alternative at all. It is nothing but madness.

Immediate priority should also be given to greatly expanded sharing of our material resources. We have been blessed in incredible abundance by God and although we comprise only a small minority of the world's people, we own and consume an overwhelming percentage of the world's resources. As in all true charitable giving—and our responsibility to less fortunate people is at least as much a matter of justice as it is of charity—we must give from our substance rather than from our surplus.

A third priority is the development of a mentality of conservation in ourselves. In recent years, since we have been gravely inconvenienced by the threat of dwindling oil supplies, conservation has become trendy. It has come to be fashionable to do with less, "to reduce," as they say on the suddenly public-spirited oil company commercials, "our dependence on foreign oil." But conservation should mean much more than that. Conservation is the opposite of consumption and our national leadership should have the guts to present conservation as an American ideal in opposition to the spend more, buy more, use more of everything economic merry-go-round that gives the illusion of widespread prosperity while leaving almost all of us a little poorer. If we can sell electric toothbrushes and eight-passenger vans to two-member families, we ought to be able to sell conservation. And I propose that the President enlist some of the country's best creative minds and subsidize them with some of the money we would have spent on MX missiles. I doubt that "Conservation Can Be Fun" would catch on but conservation could be sold.

Our concern for the environment ought to be renewed and strengthened. This is one area in which, I believe, we are making progress but we have miles to go before we sleep. Big industries continue to pollute our lakes and rivers; nuclear-reactor waste continues to foul our soil, an unpredictable threat to our future health; and our air, if improving, is far from clean. Let's hear it for the environment, Mr. President!

Finally, I would like to hear from our president, early and often, a clear, persuasive statement of the ideals that ought to shape our future. And toward that end I suggest that a small group of people who are really the best and brightest should be commissioned to draft such a statement. This group should not be a "balanced" slate with *pro forma* representation of every which group. It should rather be composed of people who have demonstrated imagination as well as integrity, boldness as well as accomplishment, courage as well as prominence. When this group has done its job, its report should not be filed. It should be promulgated with all possible vigor from "the bully pulpit" of the presidency.

I, none too humbly, submit these proposals to the careful attention of the President of the United States.

The morality of birth control:
Unfinished business?

A great many American Catholics looked on with unusual interest as bishops from all over the world met for their biennial synod in Rome in 1980. Their high degree of interest arose from the fact that the subject of this synod was the family, not some tired, old, intramural question such as "how many auxiliary bishops can fit on the head of a pin?" The family question that undoubtedly provoked the most interest among American Catholics was birth control and the bishops of the Synod obliged by discussing it, apparently at some length. But even many of those who expected little, who knew that no basic change in the official Catholic position regarding birth control would emerge from the Synod, were terribly disappointed. On the day that Americans adjusted their clocks to the end of Daylight Savings Time, the Synod issued a statement that set the clock back immeasurably.

The first news that came out of the Synod was encouraging. Archbishop John Quinn of San Francisco gave from the floor of the Synod a statement on behalf of the American bishops. In press reports it sounded distinctly pastoral rather than legalistic.

"In the United States alone," Quinn said, "nearly 80 percent of the Catholic women use contraceptives while only 29 percent of American priests are reported to believe that contraception is intrinsically immoral." "Rejection both theoretical and practical of the church's teaching on contraception is widespread" and quoting the words of Pope Paul VI he reiterated that contraception "is an immense field to which the magisterium of the church could and perhaps should return with a fuller, more organic and more synthesizing exposition."

Although Archbishop Quinn stressed that he was not "attacking the doctrine of the church," headlines in the American press made it seem like he had. He had, rather, called for the creation of a new context for the teaching on contraception. Perhaps more important, Quinn asked for the establishment of a dialogue between theologians and the Holy See on the issue of contraception. "The purpose of this dialogue should be to probe the church's teaching more profoundly."

This kind of enlightened talk from one of the Americans who are respected in the Roman Curia for their material rather than their intellectual contributions sent a shiver of apprehension among the troglodytes who rally round the motto of one of their (late) members, "Always the same." One of their members, Cardinal Pericle Felici, thereupon rose up to smite this bumptious barbarian from the West. Denouncing Archbishop Quinn for advocating morality by majority vote (a charge that was grossly untrue), Felici trumpeted, in effect, "Roma locuta, causa finita," "Rome has spoken; the question is closed."

Unintimidated by Felici, Cardinal George Basil Hume, Archbishop of Westminster, England, made what may have been the most pastoral intervention of the Synod. Recognizing that some Catholics "have no difficulty in accepting the total prohibition of artificial means of contraception," Hume pointed out that "others cannot accept the total prohibition of the use of artificial means of contraception, where circumstances seem to make this necessary or even desirable. Natural methods of birth control do not seem to them to be the definitive and only solution."

The interventions of Cardinal Hume and Archbishop Quinn were widely applauded not only by many of the people most concerned, married Catholics of childbearing age, but by a broad spectrum of theologians and pastors. These people who understand the often cruel dimensions of the birth-control question welcomed what seemed to be rays of light and hope. But their applause and hope may have been premature.

The pendulum swing back to the status quo began when Archbishop Quinn, quite rightly, went public to announce that many of the headlines reporting his synodal intervention misrepresented what he had said. But, implicitly or explicitly, this explanatory statement was a retreat from his (and the U.S. bishops') earlier statement. Something had happened in the interim. Was it Felici's arrogant denunciation? (Not likely.) Or had the American delegation to the Synod heard unhappy noises from more conservative bishops back home? (Quite possible.) Or, more likely, had the mind-set of the Synod itself, as reported by Kenneth Woodward in *Newsweek*, discouraged digression?

"Theoretically," Woodward wrote from Rome, "the Pope had invited his fellow bishops to speak their own minds. Yet from the outset, the atmosphere of the synod inhibited free debate on contraception. Although many of the church's most distinguished theologians do not accept the reasoning of *Humanae Vitae* (Paul VI's letter on birth control), no dissenting scholars among the synod's theological advisers were invited. And lest any of the Jesuit bishops, theologians, or journalists at the Synod misunderstand the Pontiff's purpose, Pedro Arrupe, the Jesuits' Father General, warned them at a Rome reception not to criticize the Pope—or the synod itself."

And so, tortuously, the Synod wound down producing a final statement that left less room for scholars to look for new meanings, for theologians to propose new solutions, and, perhaps most important, for pastors to remand this often racking question to the increasingly informed consciences of the only people birth control affects.

I am not one who believes that celibate men

cannot be perceptive and understanding in matters of marital sexuality. Just as well-informed white people are often able to empathize quite well with the prejudice and discrimination that blacks experience, priests (and bishops) who listen with openness, in confessionals and out, can fully understand the anguish that many conscientious Catholics feel when confronting the birth-control question. But I fear, alas, that these enlightened priests and bishops are not in the driver's seat in places like the Synod.

There were exceptions, of course, like Archbishop Nicholas Fernando of Sri Lanka who, according to *Newsweek*, "took the floor to issue a dramatic challenge. Unless the assembled church fathers found some realistic way to help Roman Catholics comply with the church's ban on contraception, he warned, the bishops themselves would stand convicted—like the Pharisees in Matthew's Gospel—of 'laying heavy burdens on men's shoulders' without lifting a finger to help them."

The Synod's final statement was not only dreary and depressing for many Catholics, it was, in part, silly. It blamed birth control for a host of evils: abortion, euthanasia, divorce, almost everything but psoriasis and stopped-up-drains in the home. A reader of it could look in vain for the down-to-earth practicality of the views expressed by Cardinal Emmet Carter, Archbishop of Toronto, in an interview before the Synod.

Referring to Pope Paul VI's 1968 letter reaffirming the official ban on contraceptives, Cardinal Carter said:

"The bishops knew many would not accept this ruling and so they said, 'Look, this is an ideal but if you can't accept it in good conscience it doesn't mean you aren't a good Catholic or are excommunicated.'

"The Synod (he predicted correctly) won't even recommend a change. People will have to realize there is a difference between saying, 'I know this is what the church says but I can't practice it for practical reasons' and saying 'the church has no right to tell me this so I quit.'

"If a person studies the ruling and can't obey it, then he or she will have to say that for them it is a matter of conscience. A good Roman Catholic should want to obey, but if they can't, they have to resolve it as best they can. This is not dissent from the church, in my view."

The so-called traditional teaching regarding birth control represents a terribly short-tradition because it is only in the past two centuries that the church (along with the rest of the world) really came to know much about human conception and reproduction. In this century, the church began to teach that the so-called rhythm method of periodic continence was the only moral method of birth control. It helped, of course, that rhythm was wildly unreliable and even completely impractical for some couples. It wasn't all that difficult to permit a form of birth control that became known with sad irony as "Vatican roulette." More recently, a new method known as Natural Family Planning has gained a certain popularity among Catholics. And, irony of irony, new research has found this method to be "statistically as effective in preventing conception as the Pill."(!)

Is it surprising that millions of Catholics find the distinction between these "natural" methods of birth control and other methods to be a distinction without a difference? Humpty Dumpty in *Through the Looking Glass* said, "A word means just what I choose it to mean," and establishment theologians say that certain methods of birth control are natural and others are not because they say so.

If you scratch the surface of these unpersuasive arguments, you will be told that certain methods of birth control are natural because they are "according to the natural law," an explanation that might make Humpty Dumpty clap his hands with glee. An act, they will say, is according to the natural law when it is according to the nature of the thing in question. They do not add that the nature of the thing is exactly what they (the arguers) say it is.

The church, of course, got along without "the natural law" for 12 centuries. Until Albert the Great and Thomas Aquinas came along to spell out what they found in Aristotle, the church was content to base Catholic theology on the quite different understanding of nature found in Plato and especially Augustine.

47

One aspect of the official birth-control teaching that "makes no sense" to many married Catholics is the mandate that *every act* of sexual intercourse must be open to conception. That fiat strikes them as being arbitrary, even arrogant. How much more sense it would make to teach that *every marriage* must be open to conception. Because the people who have the last word in defining Catholic moral teaching understand marriage so little, a chance to present teaching that makes sense has been lost and too many Catholic couples are not only rejecting the *every act* argument but the *every marriage* argument as well.

Judging from the statements that emerge from the policy makers on birth control, their ignorance of marriage is abysmal and they do not seem to realize this at all. The Vatican policy makers, I fear, think they understand conjugal relationship and love because they know all the facts. I say this because they hardly ever engage in serious dialogue with a broad cross-section of Catholic married couples. Several Catholic couples were invited to the Synod but there was no indication that they made any substantial contribution.

Meanwhile back in our parishes, we watch young couples who faithfully go to the considerable trouble of bringing their small children to Mass, then abstain when Communion is distributed. The reasons for their abstention can't be known but I have seen this happen too often not to believe that they are abstaining because they have been told that they cannot practice birth control and go to the sacraments.

The words of Cardinal Hume at the Synod come to mind: "It cannot just be said that these persons have failed to overcome their human frailty and weakness. The problem is more complex than that. Indeed, such persons are often good, conscientious and faithful sons and daughters of the church. They just cannot accept that the use of artificial means of contraception is intrinsically evil."

I firmly believe that millions of married Catholics believe as I do that the bishops must return to the drawing board soon. If the Roman establishment is content to sit tight, wallowing in its lack of understanding, individual pastors and bishops and especially perhaps national conferences of bishops must reach out, perhaps in the manner of Cardinal Carter quoted above, to the many beleaguered Catholic married couples who are looking for signs of hope. Our bishops should realize that their credibility is showing, that they must not continue to paint themselves into a corner on this question. There's just too much at stake.

Love means never saying "let it be"

Obviously, I need not remind you that two commandments encompass both the definition and the obligation of Christianity. Christians know that they are charged with loving God and neighbor. This, of course, is a charge that seems terribly simple but is enormously complex.

Loving God would seem to be the more difficult of the two commandments. God whom we don't see, God for whom a humanly recognizable description is lacking, God whose word and teachings must be mediated by many often fallible humans, God whom we know to be perfect and who may be expecting something of the sort from us. Loving our neighbor whom we can see and know ought to be a snap compared to the awesome responsibility of loving God. But is it?

I suggest that for people who consider themselves believers, particularly for people who practice a religion, loving God is much easier than loving neighbor. "I must love God," we say. "I go to church regularly, don't I? I praise and thank and ask his guidance in my prayers." And in the United States, at least, children in classrooms pledging allegiance to the flag, witnesses in courtrooms, businessmen at breakfasts, and even football teams in (both opposing) locker rooms invoke God with inexorable faithfulness. Despite prestigious theologians and persuasive newsmagazines, the God-is-dead school of thought just never caught on here.

Loving our neighbor, on the other hand, seems to have come a-cropper in all too many ways. We seem to find it terribly hard to live up to that part of our Christian commitment. Despite the fact that we are surrounded by countless people who desperately need our love and the help that should flow from that love, almost all of us turn our backs on people in need again and again.

Two barriers that contribute to our delinquency in the matter of loving our neighbor are easily removable. One is that we frequently lump loving and liking together. Some of the people who need our love the most are downright disagreeable, thoroughly unpleasant. Great saints are able to receive and welcome these obnoxious souls and while sanctity is the goal that all of us should strive for, most of us will have to settle for much less. But if that much less is a willingness to help those who need help, it may very well be enough for us who will never be saints.

Loving without liking then is possible, although a particularly corrosive form of dislike may eventually erode love entirely. This is the form of dislike that sets us up as judges of our neighbor's worth and allows us to parcel out our help only to those who "deserve" it. "The deserving poor" must be the most pharisaical phrase in the English language. When we help only those we judge to be worthy of help, we mock our belief in God and set ourselves up in his place.

A second, more excusable, barrier to loving our neighbor is the confusion or sense of helplessness that engulfs good people when they confront the enormity of the help that our neighbors in the world need. When we read that 6 million chidren in Africa alone are starving or on the verge of starvation, we are overwhelmed. How much can even our most valiant efforts do to alleviate this terrible problem? Sometimes, when the numbers of those suffering are not great, there are the great distances that separate us from them. If any of us was not horrified by the brutal murder of the four missionary women in El Salvador, "love thy neighbor" must have little meaning for us and yet those who were may understandably be asking, "What can I do?"

I suggest that we could begin by letting our consciousness be raised. We could inform ourselves with the background from which such atrocities arise. We could insist on getting behind the incredibly lazy and unprofessional journalism of our newspapers and television stations that writes off Third World countries as hardly worth the bother. And so while missionaries, amateur reporters if you will, have been telling us for years that there are indeed good guys and bad guys in many Latin American countries, "professional" journalists give the impression that what is happening is a Hatfield and McCoys feud between "rightists" and "leftists" (whatever the hell that means). If charged with this, these media would reply, cynically but probably truthfully, that their readers aren't interested in Latin America.

Beyond raising our consciousness with information, we can also accomplish that by involving ourselves in some small way with the suffering of others. Contributions of money help but are usually too easy to be involving. Maybe something as small as talking about the terrible murders in El Salvador on our morning train instead of last night's game between the Oilers and the Steelers. Or more, asking our pastor to include a special memorial, however brief, for the murdered women in next Sunday's liturgy. I was shocked, too, by the murder of John Lennon but when I watched the many, mass tributes to the singer, I was struck by the lack of proportion between these edifying demonstrations and our real lack of respect for the four martyrs of El Salvador.

I do not pretend that loving our neighbor is easy. It is, more often than not, difficult but it is not optional but mandatory for Christians. And those of us who call ourselves that and wish to continue to be Christians must continually examine our consciences about this obligation. If the thought of 6 million starving African children is overwhelming, think of watching the child most dear to you starve. And if the death of four women we don't know in far-off El Salvador doesn't cause your flesh to crawl, think of finding a woman you love—wife, daughter, sister, friend—mutilated and dead in a stinking open ditch.

These are our neighbors and God knows we had better love them.

Catholics are more than
a Mass movement

Catholics, obviously, are a lot of things. We
have come a long way from the catacombs when
clutching together for survival was almost all-
important. Probably more important, we have
come a long way since Vatican II announced the
end of the post-Reformation era, the era of a
church with its wagons drawn in a circle the
better to repulse the marauding heretics.

The fathers of the Second Vatican Council un-
earthed an old truth, one well known to the
church of the catacombs but buried in the rub-
ble of historical accommodation for many centuries. They announced again that all of us who
embrace the teachings of Jesus of Nazareth and
do our best to live by them comprise the church.
The church of my school days was pretty much
a "they"—the Pope, bishops, pastors—to which
"we," the rest of us, would be permitted to belong if we were good. Even then it was no longer
true that clergymen were among the few who
had an opportunity for higher education but a
structure based on the social character of a
largely immigrant church was still dominant.
The great council made us aware that this time
was past. We are (all) the church, it said. No
more "we" and "they."

This rediscovered conception of the church

brought with it a quantum increase in responsibility and not all Catholics were happy with that. Some still long for the days when "Father" told them flatly what was right and what was wrong. Some even long for the days when we could get our sackcloth and ashes ready-made, right off the racks. No flesh meat on Fridays (unless you lived in Spain). Lobster and shrimp were okay and they were affordable then even if more difficult to transport. Catholics 21 through 59 were obliged to fast. "A collation of bread or other substance not to exceed two ounces in weight is permitted at one meal and ten ounces at the second." "Does a milk shake break my fast if it isn't too thick, Father?" "What about clear chicken broth? Can I have that instead of two ounces of bread?" No wonder so many Catholics went to law school.

Today, more than likely, "Father" will answer questions by saying, "Here's what the church teaches. You're an intelligent, educated adult. You will have to put your acts in the context of your own life, I don't know you well enough to do that. You will have to square your actions with your conscience and, most important, you will be responsible and have to take the consequences of what you do." A persuasive case can be made that the last part of that advice is what bothers a lot of the yearners for the good old days. How much easier it was to do what Father said unquestioningly. If he was wrong, that was on his conscience, not mine.

So, what some critics call a new permissiveness is anything but. Catholics are coming to realize that they must take responsibility for their lives. The church is a community of believers and we are responsible one to the other and in the Confiteor of the Mass we ask God and "our brothers and sisters" to forgive us for anything sinful that we have done or good that we failed to do. We, it is very clear, are responsible.

What, then, makes a Catholic a Catholic? We, of course, recognize the Pope acting together with the bishops as the leadership of the church. That alone distinguishes us from, say, the Baptists or the Muslims. But there is obviously more to being Catholic. For one thing, we worship differently than do the members of most other religions. The Mass is unique and of the essence of our Catholic belief. No matter how badly a Mass is celebrated, how sloppy the liturgy, how dreary the music, in itself the Mass is indispensable for Catholics. (Some may have noticed that I have not mentioned the homily, which, mercifully, is not an integral part of the Mass and could, theoretically, be dispensed with. There, I've said it!)

But while the Mass and participation in it is essentially Catholic, the faithfulness at Sunday Mass may not be an unerring measure of Catholicness. Messrs. Gallup, Harris, and Roper, understandably, use regular attendance at Sunday Mass as a handy yardstick for determining who is and who is not Catholic and if measure they must that yardstick is probably as good a judge of individual "Catholicity" as any other. It could, however, be wrong.

I have known Catholics who attend Mass on almost every weekday of the year but rarely take part in Sunday Mass. A bit eccentric, perhaps, but they could hardly be called "non-Catholic." A leader among Hispanic Catholics told us recently that many Hispanics who would never miss Mass on their feast days are indifferent regarding Sunday Mass. "On feast days, we all, priest and people, celebrate together. Why should I join the priest in his Sunday boredom?"

The point, I think, is that the Catholic Church is a big, wide, often wonderful church with room for many. Many kinds of people, many kinds of celebration, many priorities. The teachings of Jesus of Nazareth are few but awesome in the responsibility they impose on us and spectacular in the rewards they promise to those who follow Him. Let's not let being Catholic confine us to mean streets. It's much too liberating, much too great a gift for that.

Red or not, bogeymen are just that

Some time ago *Newsweek's* treatment of the tragic turmoil in El Salvador featured two photos. One showed uniformed soldiers of the Salvadoran government, mostly teenagers, while the other showed ragtag "soldiers," mostly teenagers, of the rebel forces opposing the government. These, our State Department and our incredibly slothful media would have us believe, are the adversaries in an ideological struggle, rightists and centrists representing the government and leftists or Marxists opposing them. But the idea that these young people on both sides, poor and barely educated, even know what ideology means would be laughable if it were not so sad. And it is just as fatuous to believe that the leaders of these two factions give any kind of a damn about ideology. Both sides are battling for power and both, presumably, believe that they would be better for their country.

The "ideological content" of the war in El Salvador comes from outside, from cold-blooded men in Moscow and, I regret to say, from cold-blooded men in Washington. And, tragically, even this ideological content is only window dressing. Both great powers continue their struggle for control and influence throughout the world and the new administration in Washington has decided to make tiny El Salvador a showcase for its simplistic, macho foreign policy. "We'll show those Russians they can't push us around even if we have to destroy El Salvador to prove that to them." But if the voice of this policy was the voice of the former Secretary of State Alexander Haig, the hands were the hands of (can't you guess?) Dr. Strangelove himself, Henry Kissinger.

The highly respected Washington columnist, Georgie Anne Geyer, has pointed out that for a year Kissinger "has been extolling in private foreign affairs groups what now turns out to be a revealing idea."

"The United States, he has said repeatedly, should challenge the Soviets in a minor area of our choosing where we can win a quick victory.

"He said that we must choose the terrain, put in whatever power is necessary to win and thus begin to reverse the momentum the Russians have gained in the last six years.

"This U.S. challenge would have to be winnable and it must serve to turn the Soviets and the Cubans from the idea that they can get away with anything."

So, to hell with the Salvadorans. We've got bigger fish to fry. And, after all, it is us not those Third World gooks that matter!

In order to sell this chillingly cynical policy to the American public, it is, of course, necessary to sell it as a struggle between the good guys and the bad guys, the government forces in the whites hats and the rebels in the black hats who, as everyone knows, are (aha!) Marxists. It doesn't matter that Marxism is a hoax, at most a fossil, that even in 1917 Marxism was a minor factor in the overthrow of the Czar by the Bolsheviks. It doesn't matter that Marxism as a philosophy of government has never prevailed in any country unless it was or is enforced by military power. Marxism is an utter failure but it continues to be a convenient bogeyman, to rationalize completely pragmatic governmental policies.

It is meaningless in foreign affairs to think of Russia as a communist state. It is, of course, that but, much more to the point, it is imperialistic and opportunistic. It has always been the policy of Soviet Russia to make friends in other countries with whom it will, regardless of ideology. This was the foreign policy of the British Empire in its heyday and now, apparently, it is the policy of the United States. The difference between the cold-blooded pragmatism of the Russians and the cold-blooded pragmatism that has, fitfully, been American foreign policy since World War II is that the Russians have a much better record of choosing to support the forces that are likely to win out in the long run. We continue to choose the Diems, the Somozas, and the Pinochets who have the power at the moment even when the handwriting on the walls (literally) tells us that their own people will eventually reject them. Ho Chi Minh was not a

Marxist when he came to the United States in the 1950s asking us to help his peoples' movement. But when the most disgraced American in our history since Aaron Burr used his considerable influence to reject Ho, the Vietnamese turned to the Russians who, once again, picked the winner.

The point I am making is that if we intend to be cold-blooded pragmatists in foreign affairs, we had better get good enough at the game to recognize the likely winners in the internal struggles of other countries. We backed the loser in Nicaragua just as we did in Iran, Angola, and Mozambique. The men with the better guns and the helicopter gunships may hold the upper hand in El Salvador for awhile but little groups of oligarchs who exploit the poor and ruthlessly suppress even their most peaceful opponents cannot prevail in the long run. The days when that could happen have passed. And when a "popular" uprising eventually succeeds, who will be to blame if it is "Marxist"?

To say that if American foreign policy is to be pragmatic, it ought also try to be successful is not to argue that this is the way to build the best possible world. We claim to believe in God and in democratic principles of government. We ought to be repelled by policies that force military aid on a government that is unwilling or unable to control terrorists who murder opponents, Mafia-style, who assassinate the heroic archbishop of El Salvador's capital while he is saying Mass and who murder and rape women including three nuns who were devoting their lives to helping the incredibly poor Salvadorans. We should be filled with righteous anger when our selfish, cowardly, or ignorant legislators rubberstamp policies that could crush the hopes of poor people for justice in El Salvador, Guatemala, and even Nicaragua.

Tirelessly we denounce immorality in the world, in family life, on the streets of our cities, in the media, and yet once again, almost within a generation we are rushing eagerly to make another war immoral by making it our own.

Papal penmanship in a Selectric age

There are a number of differences between Catholics and other religious groups but perhaps the most visible difference is the fact that we Catholics have a pope. The other groups, of course, choose their leaders but for several reasons the papacy is a unique institution. Most obviously, the papacy is different because of its long continuity. It is different, too, in the fact that in a time when royalty has all but disappeared, Catholics, and many others as well, pay homage to the Pope in a manner reserved only for him. Presidents, prime ministers, even royalty are seldom accorded the honors we give to the Pope. Most significantly, the Pope is unique in the weight that Catholics attach to his teaching, to the words he speaks and writes.

We tend, of course, to give more weight to the Pope's written words than to those he speaks. The latter are sometimes off the cuff, so often is he required to speak, or are addressed to the particular groups (dairy farmers, bus conductors, or a high-school band from Otumwa, Iowa) that visit the Vatican. Except on those occasions when the Pope speaks formally, in concert with other bishops, his written words merit greater attention.

Every pope issues circular letters to all the faithful. We call them encyclicals and by doing so we probably reduce greatly their readership. (Perhaps we should take a leaf from the book of the governmental media manipulators, describe them as confidential letters, allow enough time for suspense to build, then leak them to a favored columnist.) But, nevertheless, they are letters almost always devoted to a particular subject.

Some of the papal letters achieve wide readership, some attract great attention, some both. The so-called social encyclicals of Popes Leo XIII and Pius XI were widely read and many of their teachings were accepted. They were fortuitous in their timing. Leo's letter strongly affirming the right of workers to organize into labor unions of their choosing came at a time when many, including Catholics, would have denied that right and the great letter of Pius XI strongly declared the right of every worker to a just wage and decent working conditions in an era when there was by no means a consensus for that view among employers.

But as is always the case when the Pope writes or speaks, the blueprint that Leo and Pius etched for social justice was not unanimously accepted by Catholics. Even today there are many Catholics who consider themselves pillars of orthodoxy who are skeptical of the main teachings of the papal encyclicals and who would blanch if they were to read the fine print in them.

Realistically, it is of the nature of papal teaching (as it is of teaching of any kind) that thoughtful people will be persuaded by some of it and not by other portions of it. The long and fruitful papacy of Paul VI provides striking testimony of this fact. Catholics who are content to ignore Paul's letter "On the Progress of People" rend their garments and all but foam at the mouth in public places if someone confesses a lack of enthusiasm for that Pope's assertion that all except approved birth control is seriously sinful. I for one find "On The Progress of People" to be almost extraordinarily creative but I know that much of it would shock the socks off some Catholics who wrap themselves in papal gold whenever their own ox is gored. It is a painful irony of this kind of inconsistency that enthusiasm for specific papal teachings is too often in inverse proportion to the degree of responsibility the teaching imposes on the enthusiast. A Catholic industrialist, for example, who might sputter with rage if he knew the responsibilities that "On the Progress of People" would impose on him will shout from the highest hill that unapproved birth control is immoral when birth control is no longer (or never was) a problem for him.

Nonetheless, it is impossible to be a Catholic without agreeing that all papal teaching deserves the respectful and careful attention of all of us. I think, for example, that it is unfortunate that some of those who dissent from the birth-control strictures of Pope Paul's letter, "Of

Human Life," as well as some of those who un-critically applaud those strictures, seem not to have read that letter in its entirety. If they had, they would have heard Paul's eloquent and joy-ous acclamation of the unitive nature of sexual expression in marriage. And to those Johnny-come-latelies who respond to that, "Big deal!" I point out that it was really only a few years ago that it was the more or less official teaching of the church that sex was a necessary evil, noth-ing more than a means to an end.

It ought also to be remembered that papal let-ters, for all the reverence due them, are letters and like all letters they speak of their times to their times. How often we come upon a letter we have received years ago and are almost puzzled by its contents. Its context has probably faded from our memory and the references are often meaningless. And how many of us would like to be held rigidly to all of the opinions expressed in such dated letters? To anyone who thinks that the ravages of time do not affect papal letters, I suggest, as only one example, a rereading of Pope Pius XI's letter on Christian Marriage. Yet this letter, almost quaint today, was a textbook in Catholic university marriage-and-the-family courses in my college days.

It is grossly unfair, I believe, even to suggest that popes, our 20th-century popes at least, are unaware of the timeliness of the words they speak and write. And as humble men they know that even though they pray that God will speak through them, they are not God. How else explain the agonized tentativeness that so many have found in Pope Paul's birth-control encyclical? This holy man, the greatest pope of our century, asking all of us to pray with him with a transcendent humility that is nearly heartbreaking, was unwilling to read anyone out of the church. *"Piano!* Go slowly," he told an impatient Hans Kung. "Come home!" he beseeched an arrogant Archbishop Lefebvre.

This, I believe, is the heart of papal teaching. The Pope asking, "Please pray for me that I may teach wisely." And, surely. we owe him our prayers.

Let them eat welfare rolls

"What's black and blue and getting bluer?" If your answer is "poor people in the United States," you're probably right. The evidence that the rich are getting richer and the poor are getting poorer is pretty persuasive. The income tax cuts that seem to be on their way won't help the poor who don't have enough income to pay that tax in the first place. And every time a state or municipality needs more revenue, it tacks a cent or two onto the sales tax, the one tax that really matters to the poor because nearly always they must spend 100 percent of their income just to stay alive.

Furthermore, it's hard to believe that the Reagan administration budget cuts will not make the plight of the poor even more desperate. The soothsaying of "the supply-side economists" explaining how the effects of what George Bush once called "voodoo economics" will eventually help everyone is of little consolation to the American poor. It's that "eventually" that sticks in their throats. A lot of the poor might be terribly thin by the time enough pie trickles down from the sky to provide any real nourishment.

The answer to the question, "Who are the poor in the United States?" shouldn't surprise any of us but it probably would. The majority are white, many are in poor health or disabled in some way, more are advanced in years, large numbers are mothers (or sometimes fathers) with a houseful of small children to care for, and finally there are a sizable number with no needed job skills. One of our prominent political leaders remarked on the large number of Help Wanted Ads in the Sunday *New York Times* and wondered aloud why so many in New York were jobless in the light of this. If he had the read the fine print in the ads (even the large type), he would have realized that most of the ads were for engineers, computer specialists, and other highly skilled professions and that many required a college degree as a minimum.

I am not one of those who automatically objects to the discontinuation of federal funding of social-welfare programs. Despite the fact that the number of federal employees as a percentage of the total population has decreased steadily during the last 20 years, there is enormous waste in almost all governmental programs. (Ironically, of course, the most scandalous waste is in the so-called Defense Department, the budget for which our gutless legislators insist on expanding apparently in the belief that the way to discourage the Russians is to throw money at them.) But all things considered, there is no absolute reason why the *federal* government must solve all the social problems of our nation of 220 million. There are other governments—state, county, city, and village—and there are private institutions and entities that could and should look to the needs of the poor and the powerless. Almost forgotten, of course, in this equation are the countless millions of more fortunate Americans who could, if they would, help others on a neighbor-to-neighbor basis.

But the flaw, possibly tragic, in the current hasty scuttling of federal social-welfare programs is the cold-blooded indifference that seems to underlie it. From the point of view of political science, decentralization of such programs makes sense. Layers of bureaucracy ought to be removed and funding such programs closer to their needs ought to be (and oh how the Reagan people love this phrase) more cost effective. However valid this reasoning, it ignores the reason why most such federal programs were instituted in the first place. Smaller entities—states, cities, private groups—were not meeting the needs of the poor and, as a result, the federal government began to act.

A plausible case can be made, I think, that a program of placing social problems on many more doorsteps, of decentralizing the responsibility for meeting the needs of the helpless needy, could eventually (there's that word again) be healthful for our whole society. But what are those in need to do in the meanwhile? Pray, of course, but even God does not promise to answer all prayers immediately.

What I miss in the pronouncements issuing

from Washington on this subject is a sense of compassion. I wonder if President and Mrs. Reagan even begin to realize what the lot of the poor in America is like. I wonder if Mr. Stockman or Senator Baker ever have sleepless moments of concern for mothers in our urban and rural ghettos reacting in agony when their children say, "I'm hungry." None of this is exaggeration and if any of those well-intentioned people doubt my word, I will gladly take them by the hand and show them the evidence.

I think we have reason to believe that most Americans are no longer interested in the ideals that nourished the origin of the United States, ideals that made us responsible one for the other with deep compassion for those less fortunate than we.

Confession: Is it in Limbo?

Some time ago the cover story in *U.S. Catholic* was called "10 reasons why Catholics have stopped going to Confesson." The author of the article had talked with a variety of Catholics, priests, religious, and lay, and asked them why they thought the number of American Catholics approaching the Sacrament of Penance had diminished so greatly. As the article title indicated, the reasons given tended to fall into ten categories.

But if the diminished "popularity" of going to Confession was unquestioned, the popularity of the subject was significantly intense. Copies of the issue featuring the article disappeared rapidly from church and other racks. The fact that Confession continues to be a "hot" topic among Catholics came as no surprise to the people who pay attention to such things. At Claretian Publications, for example, books and pamphlets about Confession have been sales leaders consistently for the past 15 years. How then can we account for the pervading interest in what is now called the Sacrament of Reconciliation and the ebbing willingness to participate in the sacrament?

I think that this paradox arises from the gap that most Catholics feel in their lives now that they have backed away from Confession because they found it wanting in many respects. Trained from childhood to "go to" Confession to recite a grocery list of sins, many Catholics came to find this kind of moral bookkeeping meaningless. Long unhappy with kneeling in a dark closet to mouth all-too-familiar sins to an unseen presence, many Catholics said "Enough!" Not a few Catholics bear scars from the verbal lacerations of insensitive confessors. (Almost every Catholic has a favorite Confession horror story, some humorous, some bizarre, some teeth-grinding.) But for all this, most Catholics feel deeply the need for an encounter, a ceremony, even a confrontation that will heal. All of us know that we are fallible and weak and all too susceptible to the temptations of the world, the flesh, and the devil. All of us fall from grace from time to time and when we do, where do we turn?

In recent years, the church has tried to address these needs by restating the theology of the sacrament (as well as renaming it). It created a new formula whereby penitents have the option of meeting with a confessor, face-to-face, in a reconciliation room. Careful instructions were given to the ministers of the revised rite. They were not to be confessors in the old sense; they were, for example, to pray together with the penitents. They were not to be psychological counselors though the temptation to be such may have been overwhelming to more than a few ministers.

The revised rite of reconciliation was inaugurated in all American Catholic parishes with considerable fanfare several years ago. In most parishes, formal instruction on the subject was given from the pulpit on three successive Sundays. And then, it seems, the subject was dropped in far too many parishes.

I regret that the *U.S. Catholic* article I discussed above did not attempt to determine the reconciliation practices and experiences of parishes in the United States. Data of this kind may exist elsewhere but if it does, I don't know where and I hope this knowledge gap will be remedied. But I do know that many parishes do not even offer the option of the new rite. They do not, in fact, have a reconciliation room. And frequently, even in parishes that do, little or no attempt is made to instruct the faithful in the theology of the sacrament, much less to dialogue with them about their needs and hopes.

Public penance services in our churches were to be another feature of the new understanding of the sacrament. But the willingness of some zealous pastors and even a few less-than-straitlaced bishops to end these services with general absolution caused church authorities to run scared and sound the alarm that such services were to be soft-pedaled.

Yet these public penance services would seem to be the most likely fix, at least in the short run, for the problem that obviously exists. The Catholic Church, after all, got along without oral confession for almost a thousand years until some Irish monks, probably demonstrating the extravagantly verbal orientation of their culture, created the confessional. And who is to say that the practice of the second thousand years of the church is carved in stone more deeply than the practice of the first thousand years?

In any event, there is, I believe, a hunger among American Catholics for a sacrament of reconciliation that is meaningful to most. And it occurs to me that many of the same Catholics who are wondering what happened to Confession are asking if Catholics still believe in Limbo. If we do, that just may be where Confession is.

A mailbag of penned-up emotions

One of my more pleasant duties is the signing of letters each year to recent college graduates who have been designated to receive gift subscriptions to *U.S. Catholic.* It is pleasant for a number of reasons. It means, in the first place, that presumably somewhat special young people will be reading the magazine for at least a year and that a significant number of these young readers will choose to stay with us beyond that first year. It also means that more than a few of them will accept the invitation in our letter to them to carry on a continuing conversation with the editors of *U.S. Catholic.* Almost immediately, we begin to receive letters that are bright and imaginative, offering fresh perspectives that challenge us. Each letter we receive, moreover, helps us to keep in mind the fact that our readers are individuals, not merely 56,000 or so units.

Reading all of the mail from our readers is, for the most part, a labor of love. We do, of course, get some crank letters, even hate mail. One interesting fact about the kind of venom drippers that are written with crayons is that they invariably come "Postage Due." One shouldn't be surprised, I suppose, that the kind of nut who writes this kind of message is also a cheapo. But, on balance, our mail is overwhelmingly positive and in this category I include the good letters from readers who, with thoughtfulness, take exception to some of the things we've said.

If I had to characterize the bulk of the letters we get from priests, religious, and our predominantly lay readers I would describe it as open. Open to the new, open to change, open to creativity in adapting the old and traditional to the turbulent times in which we live. In these letters there is often an awareness that many of the problems that we face today are of a kind that have never before confronted humankind. Even our parents and grandparents were not required to sort out the moral issues of nuclear war or the poisoning of the environment or of maintaining family life in the centrifuge of popular culture.

Quite obviously not all of the letters we receive occasion joy. The crank letters, already mentioned, make us laugh but there is another small minority of letters that can only be called sad. These few are those that conceive of our Catholic religion as a kind of straitjacket, something akin to the wet sheets that once were wound around mental patients to keep them quiescent—because they couldn't be trusted to act responsibly on their own.

This crabbed and confusing conception of Catholicism is a caricature of even the kind of religious understanding that prevailed before the Second Vatican Council. Those of us who remember that time know that the parodies so popular in print and on the stage today are grossly oversimplified. For every Sister Flakey that most pre-Vatican II Catholics remember, there were dozens of dedicated women doing an exceptionally good job teaching and directing kids. And for every Father Pomposity preening and/or fuming from altar and pulpit, there were many intelligent, decent men doing remarkable things under often impossible conditions.

There was far more openness in the church then for those who sought it than we sometimes recall. I doubt that there would have been as many survivors as there obviously are if the prevailing Catholic mores of the time were really obsessed with the likes of reflecting patent leather shoes.

But unfortunately some Catholics continue to cut their religion down to a size they feel comfortable with. These are the people who look back nostalgically to a religious life that never was—not at least in the memory of any living person. These are the letter writers whose priorities are so skewed they can't distinguish the varnish from the wood. They, quite understandably, hold up Mother Teresa of Calcutta as a saintly model, then in the next breath tell us why she is a worthy role model. Not because she takes "the wretched refuse" of her country into her hospices without question or compensation but because she continues to wear her nun's habit.

I find these letters sad because the richness and creative diversity of Catholicism seem to have escaped their writers. To them, sadly, the religion they profess is a collection of little laws and starchy customs. They seem to have memorized the six precepts of the church while failing to recognize the beauty in the life and witness of Jesus.

But don't get me wrong. Keep those letters and postcards coming. The brickbats as well as the bouquets. Even those crayon-written messages marked "Postage Due."

Devilish answers from a
godless religion

As I write this I have just watched the annual all-star baseball game. But never fear, I am not preparing to discuss sports in America. I am concerned rather with the rituals that preceded the game.

The ball that was to be thrown out to open the game was delivered by a military paratrooper from Fort Bragg who parachuted onto the playing field. The ceremonial first ball was thrown out by Vice-President George Bush who believes that we can win a nuclear war if we can hold down American casualties to less than a hundred million. And when the soloist of the national anthem reached the words, "the bombs bursting in air," the sky was filled with exploding rockets.

Earlier on the day of the game I had learned that 11 and 12-year-old boys at a Boy Scouts of America camp were being taught to use rifles with guns and targets supplied by the National Rifle Association.

In the interest presumably of encouraging thrift, the NRA did not donate the bullets used. They merely subsidized the sale of these, five bullets for a dime! (Some of the boys will be terribly shocked when they join street gangs a few years hence and discover that bullets cost considerably more than that.)

Please God, there is less to all this than meets my eye. I sincerely hope so. But anyone who knows the history of this century is bound to be concerned, maybe even alarmed.

One of those who is "worried about our drift toward a fascist state" is Bishop Maurice J. Dingman of Des Moines, Iowa. "I see so many omens that remind me of my experience in Italy as a seminarian during those hectic years, 1936-40, just before the beginning of World War II," Bishop Dingman wrote recently.

"I see a catering to the fears of people and a growing emphasis on law and order and the consequent theme of 'security.' The New Right seems intent on driving a strategic wedge between the middle class on one side and the labor unions and the poor on the other.

"Are we drifting into a state of mind in which we find opposition to communism resulting in acceptance of fascism as an alternative?"

Fascism in Nazi Germany and in Mussolini's Italy began as exaggerated patriotism. Love of country, surely a virtuous sentiment, was gradually and almost unnoticeably built into a civil religion. With the aid of quasi-religious rituals and liturgies, respect for one's country becomes worship of one's country. The German people, after their devastating losses in the first World War, felt disgraced and humiliated and provided a fertile soil for the ne'er-do-well house painter and his cohorts who promised "tomorrow the world." After Vietnam, Watergate, and the hostage debacle in Iran, many Americans feel embarrassed and are all too ready to genuflect before an altar of a civil religion based on a macho, I-can-lick-any-kid-on-the-block philosophy.

There are other parallels between the present state of the United States and that of pre-World War II Germany. The economic devastation and runaway inflation in Germany during the 1920s and early 1930s led to great concentration of economic power in the hands of a few giant corporations. The barons who controlled these monopolies were all too willing to climb into bed with Hitler. His plans for worldwide militarism provided lucrative contracts for Krupp and I. G. Farben and these opportunists discovered too late that the Feuhrer had debauched them.

Bishop Dingman, who is one of the leaders of the National Catholic Rural Life Conference, is one of those unhappy about the growing concentration of economic power, with the apparent blessing of the federal government, in the United States.

"The El Salvador problem," he wrote, "reminds me that we are drifting toward a situation very similar to that beleaguered Central American country. Fourteen families own the bulk of land in El Salvador. Are we drifting toward a situation in our own country where 14 corporations will own the bulk of our agricultural land?"

Noting that "the big get bigger (and) the conglomerates continue to increase their holdings," the bishop said, "I am upset also by the language that is used. Food is likened to oil and is referred to as 'a worldwide negotiable commodity.' It is scary when a big oil company broadens its diversification by entering the food business. What are the moral implications?"

Regardless of the frequency of its incantations and pseudo-prayers, a civil religion is by definition godless. And such a religion can flourish only in a vacuum created by the default of God-centered religions. Bishop Dingman and, I am sure, other religious leaders are trying to fill that vacuum. But more than the perceptiveness of a few leaders is needed. The consciousness of many people of good will must be raised to an awareness that nothing of God's creation is ours to own and to do with as we please.

In "this moment of truth," Bishop Dingman reminds us that "all of us are strangers and guests upon the land. Our response must be prophetic as we become lighthouses in a world that needs the light of faith."

Piety is not a dirty word

One of the problems with a living language is that words keep changing their meanings and some of these, in the process, deteriorate in value. One such word is "pious."

The primary definition of "pious" is "marked by or showing reverence for deity and devotion to divine worship." "Pious" also means "dutiful, virtuous or deserving commendation." Nothing wrong with that, is there? But the same dictionary also offers these alternate meanings: "marked by conspicuous religiosity" and "marked by sham and hypocrisy." That's a broad spectrum of meanings.

Ask yourself if you would be complimented if someone described you as "pious." Most of us probably would not be; yet there is no other word to describe this indispensable ingredient of sanctity. And aren't we all called to be saints?

I thought of this when I read that, some time back, Cardinal James Freeman of Sydney had appealed to Catholics to close what he called "the piety gap." In a sermon to the Australian Catholic Women's League, the cardinal describes the piety gap as "ignorance among a whole generation now growing up of many of the once popular devotional practices that have been discarded, without anything being put in their place." A point very much worth making.

There are, I think, two constituent elements in piety that make its neglect or absence particularly impoverishing. The first of these is that pious practices tend to involve the whole person, not just the mind. During the years that most of us were growing up, piety sometimes ran out of control. Pious devotions, prayers, hymns, articles spilled over into sentimentality and mawkishness. In time there was an inevitable reaction that purged out the old leaven with such astringency that we were left with something pure and terribly cold. Anything, it seemed, that appealed to the senses must be discarded. The error of our old ways was pointed out with indisputable logic and prayer and worship became solely functions of our newly cleansed intellects.

But we are creatures of both bodies and souls. David, we know, worshipped God by singing and playing his harp. We sing while worshipping, of course, but in our reaction to the saccharine, often banal words of the old hymns, we substituted lyrics so theological that they preempt our attention at the expense of music.

In reaction to the excesses of piety we also pinched out many well-loved and entirely respectable devotions. Our motivation was laudable. We wanted to emphasize the unique importance of the eucharistic liturgy, the Mass. We wanted to make sure that the Mass was not just the center ring in a three-ring extravaganza of prayer. What we did not foresee was the gap that Cardinal Freeman spoke about. The Mass, terribly correct but often dry and uninvolving, and private prayer proved not to be enough for many Catholics. Many Catholics miss the warmth and, if you will, the sensuousness that they remember of Benediction of the Blessed Sacrament, Forty Hours, May processions, and novenas. They believe that they ought to be trusted to keep these pious devotions in proportion, properly subsidiary to the Mass.

Cardinal Freeman also emphasized a second and less obvious element of piety, generosity.

"Many good people," he said, "have ceased to be really generous in the practice of their religion and have in fact reduced the practice to a minimum, while children growing up are tending to think that the minimum is all that is required."

We are not accustomed to characterizing piety as generous. We probably tend to think of the pious person as acting, if not selfishly, on his or her own, then extraorbital from the rest of us. But second thought should lead us to realize that the pious are those ready to go the extra mile, to fill the spaces that so many of us leave.

Cardinal Freeman asked us also to remember that "between those who believe and those who have ceased to believe, there are many people who in their own way are searching for God. Those people are helped immeasurably when they see people who not only believe but who express their belief in generous practice."

Piety, I think, deserves a better press. After all, some of our best friends—Francis of Assisi, Jude, Thomas More, Anthony Claret—were pious.

The leadership you follow may be your own

We Catholics have done a rotten job, over the years, of explaining to ourselves what it means to belong to the Catholic Church. Until at least the Second Vatican Council, "membership" for most of us has meant giving lip service to a body of teaching and observing a number of rules. I say "giving lip service" because we all have a tendency to pick and choose from among the teachings of the church. The more remote from our lives the teachings are, the easier they are to accept. None but a few fussy theologians have trouble accepting the doctrines of the Trinity or the Immaculate Conception. It's a little like joining a movement to denounce South Africa. Most of us will never come within 3000 miles of South Africa and hardly any of us even know a citizen of that country. But when a cause or a religious teaching impinges on our lives, acceptance may be anything but automatic.

The Catholic Church, for example, has taught for many years that racism is a sin but acceptance of this teaching has come very slowly. Even today, after decades in which the church has spoken out strongly on the subject, more than a few faithful, church-going Catholics continue to hold racist prejudices and act on them without a qualm.

The difference, of course, is that we are involved day-to-day with people of other racial, ethnic, and religious groups. In this marketplace, it is difficult for some Catholics to observe Catholic teaching. At the other end of the spectrum, doctrines such as that of the Trinity aren't very important to us personally and can be accepted with ease.

But when the Holy Spirit and all the Catholic bishops of the world assembled in Rome in the early '60s a profound change in our understanding of what the church is took place. Or perhaps I should say a change in what our understanding should be was taught by the Council. Somewhere along the line, the words of the *Confiteor* were changed dramatically. We began to confess our sins not only to God as in the past but to "our brothers and sisters" in the church. (I wonder how Michael the Archangel and John the Baptist took the news that we would no longer be confessing to them by name.) This change in emphasis, although it harked back to the spirit of the early church, could not have been more profound. We confess to our brothers and sisters and ask their forgiveness to help us to realize that they and we, all of us, not just the pope, the bishops, and our pastors comprise the church.

While it may give us a nice, warm feeling to be able to say "we are the church," the other side of the coin is that realizing that the church is the people of God imposes a lot of responsibility on all of us. But old habits die slowly and we continue to look to the bishops or to "Father," the pastor, to tell us how we should think and especially how we should act. When the Pope, the bishops, and our pastors provide leadership we should, of course, count our blessings. We should greet their advice with respect and appreciate their concern for the welfare of the whole church. And if, invariably, we wait for such advice, we will often be frozen in immobility and too often we will bring up the rear when people of good will are advancing toward goals of justice and righteousness.

Very early in the war in Vietnam, for example, Pope John XXIII deplored this terrible conflict and in the year of his election to the papacy, Paul VI began a long series of pleas that that terrible war be ended. But the American bishops, unlike the two popes, were slow to speak out. They may have been mired in the doctrinaire anti-Communism and jingoism that persuaded so many Americans that our cause in Indochina must be just. But fortunately many individual Catholics—priests, religious, lay people, even a bishop or two—assumed leadership, some risking much, and appealed again and again to the conscience of Americans. Happily the American bishops did eventually issue a strong denunciation of that immoral war but in this instance, they were followers, not leaders. I do not say that critically. It is, I believe, a strength of the post-conciliar church that leadership can come from every "level" of the church.

Paradoxically, I was moved to these remarks by a consideration of the splendid leadership that bishops are providing in many parts of Latin America. In El Salvador, Nicaragua, Brazil, Chile, and Argentina, Catholic bishops have recently stood up to despotic governments on behalf of the poor and the powerless. In countries where critics of governments are known to disappear without a trace, or die in a hail of bullets on a lonely road, such leadership requires heroic courage. But these selfless men believe, evidently, that preaching the gospels without speaking out for the powerless would be hypocritical.

We should salute the bishops who lead so well but we have no right to wait for them when injustice abounds. Leadership is our job as well as theirs.

Peace on earth: Our last chance

Everyone (well, almost everyone) is opposed to war and wants peace in the world. Yet, if this is so, why are nearly all the nations on earth preparing for war so enthusiastically? Why are the major nations careering pell mell toward the suicidal destruction of nuclear war? If this madness were confined to those states in which dictatorships ruthlessly suppressed dissent, it might be easier to understand. But it prevails in democracies such as our own, too. Freely chosen governments are just as exuberant in fleeing to Armageddon as are those whose leaders make their own laws.

The conventional wisdom, of course, is that we are not preparing for war. We are rather preparing to avoid war, the reasoning being that a weak nation invites conquest by an aggressor while a strong nation keeps aggressors, fearful of our reprisals, at bay. But this reasoning ceased to make sense when the United States and its potential enemies entered the nuclear age. This reasoning may have made sense when an aggressor could impose its troops via landing craft on the shores of its principal adversary as we and our allies did in World War II or when an aggressor shares a land border as do the Soviet Union and China. But that kind of war is an anachronism. Even with a million incredibly well-armed troops and complete control of the air and the seas, the United States could not overcome the forces of tiny, divided Vietnam. And to suggest that Russia could overrun western Europe or China without provoking an intercontinental nuclear catastrophe is naive.

That last reality is the only reasoning about war that *does* make sense as we enter the 1980s. With the exception of the horror at Hiroshima and Nagasaki, we have escaped nuclear war until now. But it is idiocy to believe that there can ever again be a major war that will not be nuclear. It is also idiocy to believe that anyone could win a nuclear war. We lost the war in Vietnam with more than 50,000 American deaths, innumerable deaths among our allies, and a financial drain from which our economy has never recovered. Yet the war itself never touched us here. Not a single American civilian was even grazed by a bullet or singed by napalm. Not one building in the United States, not so much as an abandoned garage, was destroyed. But it is utter nonsense to expect such immunity to continue if the United States is involved in another major war.

Consider this scenario: Where will you be if the warning comes that enemy nuclear missiles are on their way to targets in the United States, arrival time less than one hour? If you are at your place of employment, how far away will the rest of your family be? If you are a mother of small children, will you be able to reach them before havoc strikes? In either case, will it be the members of your family who will be among the pitiful refugees streaming down roads on foot, many horribly burned, all oozing life fluids from ulcerated skin? Or will you and your family be among the fortunate ones who will suffer a terrible but mercifully brief death from breathing superheated air that fatally sears the lungs or, indeed, from having no air at all to breathe?

Even the most hawkish of our legislators and military admit that we have the capacity to kill every Russian many times over (and that they, of course, have the same capacity to kill us). To go on manufacturing more and more even deadlier weapons is madness. To do this willingly as we are is grossly immoral, a fact that should ring out again and again from every American pulpit.

Mere rhetoric whether from pulpits or from these pages is pitifully inadequate unless it leads to action. And the action it must lead to is disarmament and if we claim to be a moral people, it must begin with us regardless of what the Russians or the rest of the world does. "Let there be peace on earth," we sing in our churches, "and let it begin with me." If we mean those words, we will say, "The buck stops here!" and vow to never again make a nuclear weapon.

"No more war, never again," Pope Paul VI told the United Nations. He knew too well that continued building of nuclear armaments will lead inevitably to nuclear war and that a nuclear war can only be the end of our world.

Who speaks for the church?

"I am the state," said the Sun King, Louis XIV of France. No pope, fortunately, (at least no modern pope) has claimed that he is the church. Popes recognize this even if many faithful Catholics do not. And this makes for some confusion in the body Catholic.

Using any yardstick, the visit of Pope John Paul II to the United States (and to Ireland) was an extraordinary event. That it happened at all was extraordinary. The only previous visit here by an incumbent pope was that of Paul VI but his visit was limited to his eloquent address to the United Nations and a Mass in Yankee Stadium. Boston, Chicago, Philadelphia, Washington, and Des Moines had never before received a pope. And the present pope is unquestionably a vibrant personality, one who has an exceptional gift for communication. Given these circumstances, it's not surprising that the substance of the words he spoke here was often smothered in the show-biz hoopla with which over-anxious locals surrounded the Pope's visit.

The media made much of the fact that John Paul reiterated the teachings of his predecessors in matters such as abortion, contraception, homosexuality, divorce, and the ordination of women. But sex is the Great American Preoccupation and you can hardly expect American media to give equal time to the Pope's words on ecumenism, concern for the poor, and disarmament. Oddly enough, his words on the sex-related questions were hardly news at all. They would have been "big" news only if he had departed from the position of his predecessor.

Catholics, of course, in this century at least, have consistently reserved the right to pick and choose from among papal teachings. And among those so reserving have been bishops and priests as well as lay people. We have heard much of the fact that many Catholics, perhaps most of those concerned, are not accepting papal teaching about birth control. We hear considerably less about the fact that in 1980, almost 100 years after Leo XIII and almost 50 years after Pius XI, there are many Catholics who have yet to accept the teachings of those two popes in matters of social justice. Or despite the fact that Pope John Paul II, Pope Paul VI, and Pope John XXIII all have pleaded again and again that the world disarm, most American Catholics would even today rush to the polls to vote against a president or legislator who favored real disarmament.

Who will say that this "picking and choosing" is not for the best? We owe the teachings of the pope respect and exceptionally careful consideration. If we take a stand in opposition to them, we must be satisfied that our position is meticulously reasoned and buttressed by the best available authorities. But that being said, Catholics believe that the Pope is infallible, that he speaks with the certainty of no error, only when he proclaims that the statement he is making is infallible. And there has been only one infallible papal statement, one that in no way impinges on the life of everyday Catholics, in the last 100 years.

All this is significant when considering the fact that responsible Catholics in many positions took exception to one or several of the statements made by Pope John Paul II during his American visit. Some who strongly favor the opening of ordination of women to the priesthood have made it clear that they believe the Pope was mistaken in this matter. John Paul was less specific in his words about divorce but devout Catholics, particularly those widely experienced in ministry to the divorced, find it hard to agree with the Pope's stated position. His reiteration of the traditional teaching concerning contraception evoked little response, possibly because most of those who stand contrary no longer consider the question moot.

I am sure that there are many American Catholics who disagree with John Paul's stand in his address to the United Nations. (I thought it splendid.) There are in fact American Catholics of a certain stripe who oppose the United Nations itself and must have deplored the recognition that John Paul II and Paul VI gave to it.

This is their right, to agree or disagree with a pope in matters that theologians are wont to call "prudential." On questions that are not part of the dogma of our religion.

I confess to some uneasiness in the Pope's approach to ecumenism while visiting here. It was not that he opposed it (God forbid!) but that his words had a tone that belied familiarity with the pluralistic world we live in. It is a far cry from a nation predominantly Catholic to a world in which the Catholic Church is a distinct minority.

But placed in a proper perspective the papal visit had a much needed importance. In this perspective, however, there is little room for jubilation over the size of crowds. In it the obvious fervor of many simple people is significant, the pomp of needlessly numerous mitered bishops is not. And it will be a long time before I forget the bewilderment of small children when they were refused Communion in their hands, the only way they had ever received.

"God writes straight with crooked lines," in the words of the now shopworn slogan. Let's praise Him for that.

Washing the glass through which we see darkly

Millions of Americans have taken a crash course in recent years, a crash course in the religion of Islam. Not only have we learned, painfully, what an ayatollah is, we have learned to discuss with at least a little sophistication the different Muslim sects, the Shi'ite and the Sunni. Like most crash courses, it has been learning the hard way but better sooner, of course, than later.

If we needed any further evidence that we are living in the midst of the greatest expansion of knowledge in the history of humankind, the realization that the once distant and still murky religion of Islam has entered our daily lives is additional proof. When we consider the knowledge breakthroughs that have occurred during the lifetime of the babies born in the years after World War II, the mind boggles.

In even the early decades of this century, the study of stars, planets, and other constellations made most of us think of anachronistic people wearing long robes and pointed hats and carrying mysterious boxes. We knew, of course, that the preoccupied people peering into telescopes in observatories on remote hilltops didn't dress that way but, to the likes of us, they might as well have. But in the last three decades, men, earth men if you will, have walked on the moon, our moon that is, and even now several of our satellites are on their way to other constellations where we hope they will photograph planets once so remote from us as to be unreal.

To date our celestial cameras and explorers have found no evidence of a planet that could support life as we know it but what once was the stuff of science fiction is now a matter for serious discussion among scientists, even among philosophers and theologians. They are open to the possibility that life could have existed on these seemingly barren stars at one time or that life may exist on them in the future when their evolution has progressed to the extent that ours has or even that they may now be supporting a type of life that is every bit as "human" as ours but unrecognizable in the light of our own earthly knowledge.

Side by side with the knowledge explosion in our physical universe, other explosions have been taking place. The quantum leaps in transportation and especially in communications have brought, for better or worse, the "blessings" of our political and economic societies to the world's most primitive people overnight. Knowledge in applied science has advanced to a staggering extent and, sadly, this "advance" is nowhere more evident than in the manufacture of incredibly cruel weapons of destruction.

Not as noticed, perhaps, has been the geometric progression in our understanding of

Divine Revelation. Although by no means limited to Catholics or even Christians, the importance to this progression of the Second Vatican Council can hardly be exaggerated. At some little distance, we now know that the Council did not begin in the 1960s and that it was the particular charism of Pope John XXIII that he appreciated the yeasting that had been going on for decades in bible studies and speculative theology and saw the need to incorporate it in the dough of the universal church.

Karl Rahner, the greatest Catholic theologian of our time, has hailed the Second Vatican Council as marking the beginning of the third major epoch in the history of Christianity. "For the Church, there was first the period of the death and resurrection of Jesus Christ and the proclamation of the 'salvation event' in "its own historical situation . . . in Israel and to it." Second came the time when Christianity "grew on the soil of paganism," primarily in Europe, after St. Paul began to preach to the Gentiles, the non-Jews. This, said Father Rahner, is a period that has continued to the present and is just beginning to change as a result of the Council.

Church encounters of the third kind

I wonder if our extraordinary belligerence in response to the challenge of that strange Iranian religious leader wasn't at least partly due to the fact that the nakedness of our ignorance had been exposed. Most of us didn't even know where Iran was, for gosh sakes. And we could have discoursed knowingly about quasars and black holes as easily as we could have discussed Shi'ite and Sunni Muslims. Aren't we supposed to be the best and the brightest, the leaders of the world in everything? How come then that this weirdo with a towel around his head can make us feel about as sophisticated as the tobacco chewers hanging around the abandoned railroad station in Foxtrot, Minn.?

The realization that there's a great, big, wide world out there, 50 miles down the pike, seems sometimes to shock. We've learned a lot in the last 50 years. About Addis Ababa in the '30s, Okinawa in the '40s, Inchon in the '50s, and Hanoi in the '60s, but we can't seem to shake the idea that the little old U.S. of A. is the center of the universe. A modern Galileo who would try to convince us that our country is only one of many moons orbiting around a great sun would get short shrift.

Our American provincialism has a lot in common with our Catholic conception of the church. Our idea of the church is so narrow and so limited to our culture and our geography that we should be embarrassed to offer it to its founder, Jesus, the son of God who created the entire universe. Catholics write angry letters to protest art that depicts Jesus as other than a 15th-century Italian nobleman and bishops wax indignant when nuns fail to dress in the everyday costume of 18th-century Belgian housewives.

In his watershed address at the Weston School of Theology, Father Karl Rahner tried to broaden our horizons and to make us aware that the church has been changing in quantum leaps in a blessed evolution toward its universal destiny. Since the Second Vatican Council, he said, the church for the first time has begun to become "a world church." This transition means that the Catholic Church will leave behind the time when it imposed in a "naive, unquestioning way . . . the bourgeois morality of the West in all its details on people of different cultures," imposed a single form of worship and a single language (even in countries where Latin had never been used), exported the tradition of Western law through the requirements of canon law, and rejected the "religious experiences of other cultures."

To emphasize the significance of this development, Father Rahner described it as the beginning of the third major epoch in the history of Christianity. The first of these, as previously noted, was the period of the death and resurrection of Jesus Christ and the proclamation of that "salvation event in its own historical situation ... in Israel and to it." The second epoch began when Christianity grew on the soil of paganism primarily in Europe, after St. Paul began to preach to the Gentiles. This, said Father Rahner, is a period that has continued to the present and is just beginning to change as a result of the Second Vatican Council.

In that period, the church acted like "a firm which exported a European religion it did not want to change, together with the culture and civilization it considered superior," he said. The congregations of the Roman Curia "still have the mentality of a centralistic bureaucracy which considers itself to know best what serves the kingdom of God and the salvation of souls in all the world and takes the mentality of Rome or Italy as its standard in a frighteningly naive way."

The Catholic Church had begun to ordain native bishops and to give up its "European mission practices" even before the Council, he said, but it was only after the Council that the "world church as such begins to act through mutual influencing of all its parts among each other."

Many questions have been and will be raised by the emergence of the church into this third period of its history and Father Rahner suggests a few. "Must the marital morality of the Masais in East Africa be that of Western Christianity or could a chieftain there, even if he is a Christian, live in the style of the patriarch Abraham?" That is to say, have several wives. "Must the Eucharist be celebrated even in Alaska with grape wine?" These are theoretical questions for the "world church," he said.

There are no easy answers to these questions, Father Rahner said, but the decrees of the Vatican Council have already made the church "no longer the church of the West with its export to Asia and Africa. . . . A qualitative leap took place." The Council opened the way for use of vernacular languages in the liturgy, letting "individual churches exist independently in their respective cultures . . . churches that despite all their relationship to Rome may no longer be ruled by a European mentality."

The changes that have occurred and will occur are comparable in magnitude to those ordained by St. Paul in bringing the church into the Gentile world. St. Paul, Father Rahner said, "proclaimed the abolition of circumcision for Gentile Christianity (and perhaps only for it), an abolition which Jesus certainly did not anticipate." Other changes were just as much a departure from Jewish origins—"abolishing the Sabbath, changing the middle point of the church from Jerusalem to Rome, far-reaching modification in moral doctrine, the origin and acceptance of new canonical writing (the New Testament)."

A crucial choice confronts us, he said. "Either

the church sees and recognizes these essential differences of other cultures for which she should become a world church and with a Pauline boldness draws the necessary consequences from this recognition or she remains a Western church and thus finally betrays the sense that the Vatican Council had."

It was also the message of Vatican II that all of us comprise the church. What we think and do as Catholics does make a difference. Especially if opening the church to all the world becomes a preoccupation of many of us.

Aren't we too big
for bedtime stories?

If you aren't aware that the Vatican Holy Office has censured Swiss theologian Hans Kung and shaken its finger at several other practitioners of the sacred science, you haven't been paying attention. The newsmagazines and newspapers were full of the matter and reaction to the criticism of Kung was predictable if not terribly distinguished.

Lined up on either side of the room were, on the one hand, the traditionalists shouting, "It's about time!" and, on the other, the liberals deploring the move. Both sides, it seems to me, have managed to skirt some of the most important issues involved. The defenders of Kung seem to be saying that while they don't always agree with Kung, it is important that theologians be given enough freedom to explore controverted questions and draw conclusions that are sometimes controversial. Kung's critics seem to be satisfied with saying that the church must speak with a single voice and his voice, it is said, differs from the "official" voice.

The declaration of the Holy Office itself isn't very helpful. Written in the kind of constipated officialese that is common to governmental bodies whether describing the foraging habits of boll weevils in cotton-growing states or deploring unauthorized withdrawals from the deposit of faith, it proclaims rather than explains. While it offers a few passing swipes at Kung's purported views on a number of theological questions, the bone that seems to have stuck in the Congregation's throat is Kung's lack of enthusiasm for the idea that the church cannot err.

But what a sadly wasted opportunity! If Kung is indeed culpable in these matters, why not use the criticism of his views to explain and teach? Why not place side by side, in language that intelligent non-specialists can understand, the teachings of what is called, sometimes disconcertingly, the magisterium and the opinions of Kung that, it is claimed, are contrary to them? With public interest already aroused, an incomparable opportunity is offered to make clear what the deposit of faith (what a ghastly expression!) really means. The opportunity could be further enhanced if one or more respected theologians would be enlisted to comment and help to explain.

It would be even better if the catechetical document that I propose began with a profession of humility. If it confessed that we, the church, have been mistaken in the past, that we are human with all the weakness that implies and that we pray that the Holy Spirit will guide us and keep us from erring in the matter before us. (A reader of such a preamble might be tempted to believe that he or she had gone to Heaven.)

Instead we are given the turgid prose of a proclamation that begins encouragingly by saying that both the magisterium and theologians have as a common end "to preserve, *to penetrate ever more deeply, to explain,* to teach, to defend the sacred deposit of revelation; and in this way to illumine the life of the church and of the human race with the light of divine truth." (Italics added.) It ends by saying that Hans Kung "can no longer be considered a Catholic theologian," an anti-climax if ever I've encountered one.

It seems to me that this opportunity to explain and teach was wasted because, if it occurred at all to the framers of the document that millions of faithful Catholics deserve a careful explanation of the matter, they concluded either that we wouldn't understand or that it was really none of our business. "Go to bed, my children. Daddy knows best."

Meanwhile "the disturbance in the minds of the faithful" that the Holy Office proclamation claims to be remedying is multiplied. I have heard it said publicly that Kung has denied the divinity of Christ but this appears to be a bum rap. Witness his statement that the criterion for the Catholic Christian "can be nothing but the Christian message, the Gospel in its ultimate concrete form, Jesus Christ Himself, who for the church and—despite all assertions to the contrary—also for me is the Son and Word of God." So wild talk abounds and confusion is compounded.

The Holy Office document is murky on this and a number of other Kung views but if there is genuine concern in Rome about "disturbance in the minds of the faithful," why not spell out, chapter and verse, what Kung has said and explain the errors that it sees?

Does anyone else find it sad that far too many curial potentates seem unaware that there are millions of educated Catholics who deserve to be treated as adults?

The Sunday sermon: A mouse that might roar

We sit in our pews awaiting, with decidedly mixed emotions, the moment. It will be a moment, we know, not necessarily of truth but almost surely one of intersection between our experience and the consciousness of the homilist. What will it be, we wonder? Will it be exhortation to be good, to live better lives? Will it be the conscientious effort of an earnest celebrant struggling to find meaning in today's passages from Scripture? Or will it be a few blessed flashes of insight, almost obviously the handiwork of the Holy Spirit?

Nothing about our religion seems to concern (bug?) our readers as much as the quality of the homilies they hear at Sunday Mass. And other serious studies of Catholic opinion have found this to be true of American Catholics generally. Most U.S. Catholics are less than happy with the quality of the liturgies they encounter but there seems to be considerable agreement that a "satisfying" homily can redeem even a bad liturgy.

If cross-examined, even the most cantankerous of critics among the pew-sitters would probably admit to sympathy for the poor homilist. We know that his task is not an easy one. Neither rain, nor sleet, nor snow can stay him from his appointed appearance, front and center, before a congregation that may seem to him to be saying, "Okay Father, dazzle me." Preparation can help, of course, and there are today many useful homily services. Some homilists run up the white flag and use these services literally but most believe, quite sensibly, that all will not be well if the voice is the voice of Father O'Reilly but the words are the words of Alleluia Publications.

More than a few of us pew-sitters have, from time to time, been exasperated enough by the inadequacy of a homily to think "Give me that pulpit. I can't do any worse." But although this may surprise many priests, most of us, honestly, would not want to trade places with them.

Before the second Vatican Council, the Sunday celebrant was free to sermonize on almost any subject that interested him and many, God knows, did. One preacher could expound the glories of Frank Leahy and the Fighting Irish as readily as another could cast withering scorn upon atheistic communism. One who was unprepared could always fall back on a rousing denunciation of filth, not the kind that pollutes the environment, but the kind that pollutes the media and the minds of teenagers.

Memorable aberrations come to mind. There was the pastor who, choking cholerically in the wings while a visiting preacher spoke in words too liberal for the pastor, mounted the just-vacated pulpit and thundered, "You have heard the words of man; now you will hear the word of God!"

And there was another celebrant, now mercifully departed from the altar, who punctuated the weekend of mourning for the assassinated President Kennedy by denouncing the late president's wife.

But Vatican II changed all that. Or at least it was supposed to. A homily, the Council Fathers decided, was to be preached based on the scriptural readings chosen for that Mass. More easily said than done but yet it made sense. The scriptural verses provide potting soil for the homilist to plant seeds, seeds that will best be nourished into live growth by the Holy Spirit. Seeds that at least will help to remedy our long-standing ignorance of the Bible.

It doesn't always work this way, of course. Some homilists, instead of meditating on the scriptural words and trying to shed light on their meaning, will use them as platforms from which to give first-grade catechism lessons. But while mine may be a minority opinion, I see light at the end of the tunnel. It may be damning with faint praise but homilies, I think, are better than they were and we're gaining.

In peroration, may I make bold to offer my friends on the other side of what once was the communion rail these helpful hints:

First, no parish ever went broke because the homilies therein were too short. Brevity in homilies can cover a multitude of inadequacies. It is possible, I admit, for a homily to be too brief if it doesn't really say anything at all. But a homilist should be satisfied if he can make one point and make it well.

Secondly, don't excoriate the saints who are present for the faults of the sinners who are absent. One poor fellow, I remember, had a weakness for deploring the sin of missing Mass to congregations of faithful who hardly every did.

Finally, try not to scold. We all have too much scolding in our lives. Young people are scolded by their parents, husbands and wives scold each other, and most of us who work are scolded by our bosses. Scolding turns us off.

Try holding the ideal of the life of Jesus up to us. Show us the wonder of that life and excite us with the prospect of our human lives led in imitation of His. In short, "Dazzle us, Father."

The sleepy faith of armchair Catholics

In the Broadway musical "Woman of the Year" the Barbara Walters-like leading character leaves a message for her secretary that she has gone to interview the Reverend Sun Myung Moon. "If I'm not back in three days," the message reads, "you can look for me in airports."

Anyone who has been in an airport in the last decade has encountered one of the intense Moonies or a zealous member of some other aggressive religious sect. Almost always young, these dedicated advocates try to press a flower, a book, or other literature into the hands of often unsuspecting travellers and ask, usually, for a donation. The latter request is an important part of these activities but to dismiss them as mere fund raising is to miss their point. Converts to these cults learn immediately that they must be *active* members and that they must do their utmost to bring others into the fold. I suggest that whatever judgment we make on the tenets of their religious belief, their zeal puts us to shame.

"Evangelization" is, of course, something new to most of us. During most of this century, American Catholics have been so busy building churches and schools that we haven't had time for much else. More often than not, our churches were built to meet a need and they filled up as soon as they were dedicated. As did our Catholic schools; and while the latter were a primary instrument of evangelization, they usually served the children of the already converted.

For a few decades in the middle of the century, convert making was "in" and a spate of books were written by celebrated converts describing their conversion to Catholicism. Some of these were interesting and helpful but others had the annoying habit of making God a junior partner on the convert's road to Damascus. We learned from these how that former wastrel or this former Communist was self-admittedly wise enough to discover the truth that others, not as bright, were willing to leave wrapped in a napkin.

But most Catholics in the United States were bullish on membership. The lines to join up were, presumably, always forming on the right. Catholics had large families and their children were baptized, made their first confessions, Holy Communions, and were confirmed without question. More remarkably, young Catholics, until 15 or 20 years ago, continued to practice their religion actively without interruption through their teens and into their adult years. It was very nearly true to say, "Once a Catholic, always a Catholic."

That situation, we know, has changed. During the '60s and '70s, young (and other) Catholics began staying away (the word "left" implies more activity than was involved) from Mass, the sacraments, and the practice of religion generally, a fact that continued to concern those who care what happens to the church.

Some time ago I wrote a piece titled, "Leave Them Alone and They'll Come Home: Or Will They?" in which I raised this question. If I remember correctly, I answered the question by coming down squarely on both sides of it. And studies done in the meantime seem equally equivocal. There is evidence that some Catholics who have dropped out in their late teens or early 20s do return to the practice of their religion after they marry and have children. But others, perhaps just as many, do not. This, I think, ought to concern us.

Quite obviously, Catholics drop out for a variety of reasons. One kind of dropout can, I believe, be spared. This is the kind of Catholic who "stayed in" only because of family ties or the nominal Catholic who "went to church" because it seemed like the thing to do. The loss of such members may decrease the quantity of Catholics but has probably improved the quality.

But far too many of the dropouts represent a real loss. These are the thinking people whose religious experience has disenchanted them for reasons that may or may not be substantial but which they are convinced are valid. There is, unquestionably, a job of evangelization to be done with this group. Some of this job will require the clearing up of misunderstandings and remedying misconceptions. Some of it will involve pointing out that "the church today is not the church you left." And maybe such evangelization requires another dimension.

That other dimension, I believe, is the flip side of the zeal exhibited by the cultists I mentioned earlier. The church, I am convinced, must demand more of its members. I am certainly not speaking of more financially or even more in terms of time and activities. It must demand more heroism, again not necessarily of the physical kind, and more sanctity. Sanctity of a positive kind, not the kind we back into by avoiding a grocery list of sins. The church should insist that being Catholic "makes a difference," that Catholics become recognizable not because we don't eat meat on Friday or do go to Mass on Sunday but because we are more charitable than most. It should insist that Catholics be recognizable because we cut against the grain of a secular culture that is for the most part anti-Christian. It must insist that Catholics comprise a true counterculture.

Just as I have argued that the greatest weakness of our vocation recruiting for the priesthood and the religious life is that we do not demand enough of our prospects and candidates, I think we often fail in evangelizing, in seeking new Catholics or in persuading dropouts to return, because we are too accommodating, more interested in satisfying than in challenging.

I believe strongly that the best and maybe even the brightest will respond only when we make it clear that there is one Christian vocation only and that is to become saints. It may be that most of us will never achieve that but if we aren't trying it doesn't make any difference whether or not we're Catholics.

Roadblocks on the yellow brick road

Some American bishops, mercifully few, are beginning to resemble the Wizard of Oz. One of these, bishop of a small Nebraska diocese, has puffed himself up and proclaimed that henceforth there shall be no female Mass lectors in his kingdom. Another who rules a minuscule Southern diocese has qualified for a comedy turn on the Tonight Show with his explanation of why there must be no female altar servers. It seems that if both boys and girls were allowed to serve Mass the boys would be so distracted they would lose interest in a possible religious vocation. (The girls presumably would lose interest in becoming nuns because they would be distracted by the boys but the good bishop doesn't seem to care a fig for them.)

You will recall that when the Wizard of Oz acted in a similarly eccentric manner Dorothy accused him of being a bad man. But he replied, "Oh no, my dear, I'm not a bad man, I'm just a very bad wizard." So it may be also in the instances under consideration. But I think I am more concerned about the great majority of American bishops who are not "bad wizards" and who surely must realize how nonsensical these sexist antics are.

Consignment of women (and girls!) to second-class citizenship is, of course, outrageous.

Mary, the mother of God, is venerated as second only to her son among all who have lived on earth and yet, had there been Mass servers when she was growing up, she would have been banned from the altar. (Banned during the celebration of Mass, that is. She would have been allowed to scrub the floor and arrange the flowers when the church was empty.) And Teresa of Avila and Catherine of Siena, Doctors of the Church, an honor given to only a handful of men, would not be allowed to read at Mass in Lincoln, Nebraska. It boggles the mind.

This arrogant discrimination against those who probably number more than half the membership of the church is surely a serious injustice. But it is also silly and sometimes comical. It is silly because there simply is no valid reason for it. Each proponent of apartheid of the sexes in the church seems to have his own "reason." I can't believe that many American bishops were not embarrassed when they read the gibberish of their brother bishops, quoted earlier, for banning altar girls. And how these good and intelligent men must have squirmed when they learned that women may no longer darken sacristy doors in Lincoln, Nebraska.

The whole scenario is comical, too, because if it were to be set to music, it would need Gilbert and Sullivan. (Although Aristophanes could probably have handled it.) The whole thing is farcical and too much subtlety would fail to do it justice. The climactic yet slapstick scene would have the hard liners fleeing to some sort of ephemeral high ground in panic while behind them, inexorably, march a band of determined women chanting a parody of "Onward, Christian Soldiers."

The panic of the hard liners, of course, is not induced by the specter of women lectors or altar girls but by their nightmare of women priests. And the high ground they think they have found is the fact that the present pope and several of his predecessors have said "No" to the ordination of women. But a long line of popes said "No" to Mass in the vernacular while the last three popes have said "Yes" to non-Latin Masses so enthusiastically that those who have refused to accept this change have become apostates.

Quite simply, equal rights for women in the church including ordination to the priesthood is an idea whose time will come if it hasn't already. And just as George Wallace barring the doors of a university to blacks and like-minded associates wearing "Never" buttons are today but sad reminders of a benighted past, those who insist that women must always walk two paces behind men in the church will rapidly become forgotten fossils.

None of this is to imply that I agree with those women who pretend to celebrate Mass in what they romantically call an underground church. Their impatience is understandable but if they insist on "celebrating the Eucharist," they are taking themselves out of the church in the same manner as Archbishop Lefebvre and his associates have in refusing to accept the only authorized ritual of the Mass.

I must note, too, that I am inclined to question the sincerity of anyone who argues for a married priesthood without at the same time arguing for the ordination of women. I say this because I have noted many who are inconsistent in this way.

Nonetheless, it would seem to be time to put aside the crabbed negativism that cuts a church of divine origin down to petty human size. Let's join together and ask God's grace that the church may be blessed with many vocations, men and women working equally for the bringing of the kingdom.

Holy Days: Out with obligation, in with inspiration

In my generation at least, one of the first catechism lessons young Catholics learned was the names and the dates of the Holy Days of Obligation. We learned to rattle these off in trim precision and with a cast-in-bronze smugness. The Holy Days were practically articles of faith. They always were and always would be. So it is no wonder that when in a 1980 survey Catholics were asked if they favored "dropping" the Holy Days or otherwise changing them, most said "No."

A majority of the American Catholic bishops, responding to the same survey, felt otherwise. They knew that attendance at the Holy Day Masses had been dropping substantially and while matters such as this are not settled by vote, it seemed obvious that a substantial number of American Catholics no longer considered missing Mass on one of the Holy Days sinful. To quote the familiar phrase that President Reagan is making infamous in quite another context, "The people are voting with their feet." Yet, when asked, many of the same group seemed to say, "Hands off our Holy Days!" Nostalgia perhaps but, whatever, the subject continues to perplex the bishops.

In recent years, of course, the Holy Days subject has sometimes been reduced to absurdity by the dithering of a few litigious bishops. Most notable have been those who worry that some Catholics will double up when a Holy Day falls on a Saturday by attending a Saturday evening Mass. The cynical explanation of this dithering is that collection revenue will be lost if such double dipping is permitted or even winked at. But I think that explanation may be too logical. Dithering for a confirmed ditherer may be an end itself, an activity that, in the ditherer's eyes, is its own justification. That, I believe, is why the dithering on this subject continues. (To cite only one example: At their otherwise splendid meeting in November, the American bishops were forced to consider a proposal that the movable Holy Days "be celebrated on Wednesdays if the date fell on Monday or Tuesday and on Thursday if the date fell on Friday or Saturday" thus avoiding "back-to-back Mass obligations." I kid you not! I swear that's what took place! The only sensible thing about the proposal was the proposing bishop's remark that "heavily scheduled Catholic laity seem to be finding back-to-back Masses more difficult to understand.")

Could we, for a minute, take a look at the Holy Days of Obligation? In the first place, with a few exceptions these days vary from one country to another. The origins of the Holy Days observed in the United States lie somewhere in church history but hardly any of us are aware of them. Why, for example, is the Assumption of Mary, celebrated in midsummer, an obligatory Holy Day when the feast of the Sacred Heart of Jesus is not? Why is Ascension Thursday one of the "days" when the feast of Corpus Christi and Holy Thursday and Good Friday are not? Why does January 1 which for many years (centuries?) was observed as the Feast of the Circumcision (now there's a feast to explain to first-graders) continue to be a Holy Day of Obligation even though it is now the feast of the Solemnity of Mary?

I suggest that we go back without delay to the nearest available drawing board and take a few positive steps:

First, drop the "obligation" altogether. If a feast is worth celebrating, Catholics ought to celebrate it because they want to and removing the obligation will force us to explain and understand the theology of the feast. If we can give ourselves a genuine understanding of those feasts we want to designate as special, we ought to be able to generate enthusiasm for them. We need only observe the intense and enthusiastic participation of Mexican Americans in the celebration of the feast of Our Lady of Guadalupe. Even those among them who are only minimally educated know the story of Guadalupe and its significance to the Mexican people. The same is true of feasts that are special to other peoples (although I don't know how much can be said for the celebration of St. Patrick's Day by most Irish Americans).

Second, we should choose as special feast days those that are not only meaningful to U.S. Catholics but which fall on days that permit a special celebration. Christmas and Easter fall into that category. To these why not add Thanksgiving and the Fourth of July? Both of these are days of national celebration and holidays for most working people. Some American parishes, in fact, already celebrate these days with special Masses with a unique liturgy and music. And why not transfer our beautiful remembrance of those who have died from November to Memorial Day enabling us to remember those who died in war *and* in peace.

The other four Holy Days of Obligation would, of course, remain on the church calendar but with the exception of the feast of the Immaculate Conception would not be considered any more special than, say, the feast of the Sacred Heart or feasts of the great saints (Joseph, the apostles, Francis, Theresa). I except the feast of the Immaculate Conception only because under this title, Mary has been declared patroness of the Americas but I admit that much would have to be done theologically and especially catechetically to make December 8 meaningfully special for most American Catholics.

Most of all, I would like to see us make these changes deliberately. I would hate to see us lose our feast days with a whimper because we gave a party and hardly anyone came.

An examination to help heal the soul

Are we who consider ourselves religious making a difference in the society in which we live? Is the influence for good of those of us who profess religious beliefs and go to church more or less regularly greater than that of those who do not? Are we satisfied that we are acting according to principles more often than in response to our prejudices?

As a kind of examination of conscience I offer here a few of the many questions that we might ask ourselves in reference to the questions above.

Item: Does it bother us to see pictures of Haitian refugees behind barbed wire fences in Florida? Is the fact that our concentration camps have no gas extermination ovens enough to excuse them?

Quite obviously, the refugee problem is not simple. Our capacity to absorb people from the rest of the world is not unlimited. But which of us is qualified to say when the limit has been reached? Who among us, encountering a single Haitian floundering in the water near a boat we were piloting, would turn away and let him drown? Or, finding a Haitian woman and her children huddling for shelter in a public building, would we call the police and insist that this family be repatriated to endless destitution in their homeland?

Cold-blooded government functionaries bypass these questions by telling us that the Haitians are not political refugees, an argument that considering the oppressiveness of the Haitian dictator, "Baby Doc" Duvalier, is questionable. But even assuming the truth of it, were the Irish, Polish, Germans, Italians, and Slavs, "the wretched refuse of (Europe's) teeming shores," who fled to the United States in the late 19th and early 20th centuries political refugees?

Item: What is our complicity in the fact that trillions of our dollars are being spent and are planned to be spent for weapons of destruction, some of them of almost unlimited lethalness, while many Americans are hungry, without decent housing or adequate medical care? Can we be content to pass the buck and say "that's for the President and the Congress to decide"? More than 50,000 American lives were wasted in Vietnam because too many of us believed that the President "knew better than we did." But we seem not to have learned from that experience.

Item: In the recent film, *True Confessions*, a wealthy businessman whose fortune was built on prostitution but who is now "respectable" is honored as "the Catholic layman of the year." Any of us whose memory spans a generation or two will know that all too often churches and other organizations of altruistic purpose are willing to accept tainted money with no questions asked if "it's for a good cause." Crooked politicians, industrial exploiters and polluters, wheeler-dealers with links to organized crime, and sleazy publishers have been able to buy "respectability" with their dirty dollars. And are we free to point the finger at the organizations bestowing such honors if we are willing to sit in the audience applauding that choice?

Item: Every decent person was horrified by the action of the Italian Red Brigade in kidnapping American General Dozier. General Dozier was rescued unharmed but, regardless, the terrorism of his captors was dastardly. But the Red Brigade is a penny-ante terrorist organization in comparison with the paramilitary assassins who have murdered hundreds, probably thousands, in cold blood in Guatemala. One recent horror committed by this group would have been almost beyond belief if it did not so closely resemble the atrocities of the Nazis. A group of men, women, and children were herded at gunpoint into a church, the church doors were locked, and the church doused with gasoline and ignited. A nun who managed to escape this echo of the Holocaust was seized and carried away to God knows what fate.

Unlike the Red Brigade terrorists, the Guatemalan assassins are under the protection of the government of their country. And that government continues to receive aid of many kinds, paid for by our taxes, with the blessings of our

President and Congress. Shouldn't this bother our consciences?

Item: Subjecting the Polish people to martial law under a military dictatorship is an outrage and deserves to be denounced as it has been by the Pope and President Reagan. But shouldn't we be just as outraged by the martial law that prevails in the Philippines and by the martial law that, just as in Poland, forbids millions of South Africans from freely walking their own streets? Far from denouncing these latter two outrages, our government praises and helps the dictators who have for a long time imposed them. Is Asian life cheaper in our eyes than European? Does the fact that hardly any South Africans vote in our elections matter?

We ought to ask ourselves questions like these. Who knows, it might just be good for our souls.

A crumbly approach to daily bread

I confess that I am worried. Maybe it's because the centennial observance of the birth of Franklin D. Roosevelt brought back vividly memories of long lines of men and women, unemployed Americans, waiting for bread and watery soup. And when the worst of our nation's unemployment problem was finally solved in the late 1930s, all of us, Republicans as well as Democrats, vowed that we would never let it happen again. Not that we could eliminate unemployment altogether, although "full employment" was our legally mandated goal, but that soup kitchens and bread lines would be all but a thing of the past.

But 50 years later, in 1982, nearly 10 percent of the men and women who want to work can't find jobs and, worst of all, the unemployment compensation floor that was supposed to keep them out of bread lines while they looked for work has disappeared or is rapidly disappearing for many of them.

Aristotle, that wise old Greek, gave a lot of attention to the need that people have to form political communities. That humans are more political than bees or other gregarious animals is obvious, he said, and the person who feels no need to live in society or is unable to must be either a beast or a god.

The logic of history also illuminates the need of men, women, and their children to reach out to other families to form an association that is both stronger and more serviceable than individual families standing alone. Such was the case when tools were fashioned from stone and crude strips of leather and such continued to be the case over the centuries as the human race became more civilized—well, more sophisticated at least.

The beliefs and teachings of the great religions, particularly Judaism and Christianity, baptized the primal urge of humans to clutch together in communities, small, medium, and large. Not only was it necessary for people to join in groups for their mutual support and protection, they were one family under God as the prophets and especially Jesus taught us to love. Yet today, in an incredible reversal of our willingness to help those less fortunate than we, we seem to be willing to abandon these poor people to the whims of fate.

It is not my intention to argue here for a particular economic system or for a particular solution to the American unemployment problem. The remedies advanced by governments in the 1950s, '60s, and '70s may indeed have been impractical or unnecessarily costly or laced with undesirable social consequences. But all of them, it seems to me, had one thing in common. All of them gave witness to the commonly shared belief that jobs must be found, created if necessary, for able-bodied men and women who need and want to work. Perhaps those jobs could be found in the private sector by using incentives such as tax reductions. Some people without even minimum skills would either be trained or put to work in unskilled jobs that would enable them to support themselves and their families, using the words of Pope Pius XI, "in frugal comfort."

What causes the worry that I spoke of at the outset is that no one in the White House or in the Congress of the United States, at least in any numbers, seems to give a damn about the unemployed. The President and some of the toadies surrounding him keep saying that there are jobs "out there" if the unemployed look hard enough for them. But anyone close to the facts knows this is not true. There *are* job vacancies but nearly all of them are for skilled, usually highly skilled, people; and most of the unemployed are anything but highly skilled.

I'm sure that the President didn't mean to be callous or cruel when he suggested that the unemployed should "vote with their feet," move to other states where, presumably, jobs are more plentiful. But jobs for the semi-skilled and unskilled are not plentiful anywhere in the United States in 1982 and Mr. Reagan demonstrates that he is out of touch with reality when he fails to realize that many of the jobless can't afford to move to the next town much less to another state.

Undergirding this frightful situation is what I see as widespread unwillingness of too many Americans to assume responsibility as our brother's and sister's keeper. What becomes of these desperate people when unemployment compensation is exhausted, when their meager funds are gone, when relatives and friends are themselves no longer able to help? There is still, some will say, welfare but welfare benefits are available to fewer and fewer and they are shrinking in some places to a point that the recipient must choose between food and lodging. They can't have both. This in the richest country in the world, where the only automobiles selling well are luxury cars priced upwards from $20,000.

Will any God-fearing person tell me that the unemployed are not our problem? Whatever the means, we must impress on our leaders that this scandal must be ended.

The reed of God continues to flourish

One of the blessings that we Catholics should be especially grateful for is the indestructibility of devotion to Mary the mother of God. Not that the history of this devotion has been tranquil. From its beginnings in the early church, it has evoked tempestuous emotions and sharply divergent opinions.

Devotion to Mary, advocates on all sides of the Marian question agree, is unique and because of this, theologian Edward Schillebeeckx tells us, "it should not be difficult to understand how it was possible for St. Paul and the saints living during the first centuries of Christianity not to show any marked devotion to Mary of the kind with which we are familiar now.

"An explicit devotion to Mary presupposes at least in part, the dogmatic development of the Marian mystery, although the more confused appreciation of Mary prevalent during the early Christian period certainly provided the latent force which facilitated the later development of Marian dogma and enabled it eventually to flourish. This indicates quite clearly that devotion to Mary, explicit to a greater or lesser extent, is an essential expression of Christian life."

Over the centuries since those early years, great theologians have disputed and even solemn councils of popes and bishops have been torn apart by debates about Mary's role in salvation history. As recently as 1963, during the first session of Vatican II, acrimonious differences on this subject among the Council Fathers made the great nave of St. Peter's ring. But, it seems, all these disputes had one thing in common. All partisans were agreed that Mary's unique role must be recognized and that she should be venerated. The disputes were usually between those who would, figuratively, at least, place Mary on a throne beside her divine son and those who wish to honor the humanity, sublime though it was, of Mary, to venerate Mary as one of us. She is, as theologian Karl Rahner tells us, "the noblest of human beings in the community of the redeemed."

Along the way the excesses of those who with the best of intentions made devotion to Mary an end in itself turned off many Catholics, particularly perhaps those who tended to intellectualize their faith and were acutely sensitive to what they felt was excessive emotionalism. And some devotees were (and are) guilty of overemotionalizing their devotion. The occurrence of numerous Marian apparitions during the past century and a half led some to embrace a terribly oversimplified theology of salvation based on the words that Our Lady was reported to have said to Bernadette at Lourdes, to the children of Fatima, and to others. Church authorities have attempted to sort out these apparitions, classifying some (Lourdes, Fatima) as authentic and others as inauthentic. A verdict of "authentic" did not mean that the church considered these extraordinary events to be true in every respect but simply that nothing had been found to judge them as untrue. Nor was anything about these apparitions judged to be a matter of faith.

Father Schillebeeckx asks for moderation in our approach to such phenomena. Speaking of those "who attain to invisible realities by means of what is visible," he points to "manifestations of popular religious life (that) are as old as the human race itself.

"No amount of intellectualism will ever succeed in eradicating them from the religious life of people. Man feels the need to stroke with his hand the rock where the Mother of God appeared. It is important for him to be able to climb, on his knees or even crawling, up the steps of the Stations of the Cross. Religion is not simply a question of the interior life. It is not a purely rational matter. Any claim that religion is exclusively rational is contradicted by Bernadette's crawling over the ground and swallowing grass and mud—and doing this on the instigation of the 'Lady' who appeared to her. These manifestations are bound to make us think of the faith of Abraham—a belief and trust in God despite all human evidence to the contrary."

Whatever the nature of devotion to Mary, it remains strong among Catholics. Blessedly strong, I would say. When in 1978 *U.S. Catholic* surveyed its readers, we found not only evidence of the strength of this devotion but its good sense. Some of the descriptions offered by the respondents might be considered less than orthodox by letter-of-the-law perfectionists but none were extreme; certainly none were kooky. Even allowing for the exceptional good sense of the average *U.S. Catholic* reader, I suspect that this kind of strong but sensible devotion to Mary is typical of the American Catholic population at large.

Contemporary Catholics seem to have successfully sidestepped what theologian Rene Laurentin calls "the two slippery paths (where) we can fall into either (excessive) 'Marian' Christianity which St. Paul would certainly not recognize as such or a Christianity without Mary that would no longer be Catholic." They seem certain that Mary—the clement, the loving, the sweet—is an indispensable part of their Catholic faith.

Marriage covers a multitude of grace

All Catholics, especially U.S. Catholics, owe a measure of gratitude to the bishop of Joliet in Illinois. Recently Bishop Joseph Imesch wiped away the egg that many of us felt was on our faces because of a particularly embarrassing "marriage case."

Two young people, one of them Catholic, approached the pastor of the local Catholic church and asked to arrange to be married there. The elderly pastor, a man who had been displaced late in life from a European country, refused their request on the grounds that the groom-to-be was irreversibly paralyzed to the extent that he could not "consummate the marriage." Both of the couple explained that they were fully aware of the young man's incapacity, that they loved each other and that they were quite willing to marry under the circumstances. But the pastor was adamant, pointing out that church law was specific, a "marriage" that could not be "consummated" was not a "marriage." An appeal to the chancery office of the diocese availed nothing but to broadcast the awkward situation as the news media learned of it and made a star of an unfortunate functionary of the diocese by interviewing him for the front pages and especially on the evening television news. I'm told that this poor fellow was cross-examined for 45 minutes by a TV crew but all the viewers saw and heard was his reiteration that the couple could not be "married in the church" because "consummation" was not possible. When this telecast returned to the studio news desk, the anchormen, usually so careful not to offend viewers in matters religious, could barely suppress their grins in the face of an explanation that seemed almost farcical.

At that point, Bishop Imesch stepped in and, using his episcopal authority to dispense, informed the couple that they could indeed be married in church. It is especially to the bishop's credit, I think, that he solved the problem pastorally, telephoning his decision to the young man, rather than issuing a statement to be read impersonally by an assistant in the traditional clerical manner.

It is unfortunately true, however, that news of what some of us consider the silliness of this situation had already spread like a prairie fire throughout the United States, and, I assume, to many other countries. By clinging to a legalism long since outdated by our growing understanding not only of physiology but, more important, of sacramentality, we, quite simply, goofed. The embarrassment we brought on ourselves was deserved.

The church, like every other institution, has goofed before and will goof again. We depend on the Holy Spirit to keep us from goofing irretrievably. But we aren't excused from trying to prevent future goofs. And I suggest that the most constructive action that we could take to preclude future embarrassment in matters matrimonial is to jettison the nonsensical idea that a marriage becomes a marriage when it is consummated sexually.

The vapidity of this definition of marriage is transparently evident when the church confronts, as it frequently does today, requests for marriage in church from couples who have been living together. The church can hardly sanction, much less bless these informal liaisons; but when the couple conclude that they sincerely wish to marry and that they value and ask the blessing of the church community, they are welcomed and their marriage is witnessed sacramentally. At this point wouldn't it be fatuous to say that the "consummation" after the sacramental invocation as opposed to the prior consummation establishes the existence of the marriage? To my knowledge, no responsible person is saying this explicitly today but implicitly this funky rationalization continues to have the rule of force.

I believe that the "consummation concept" of marriage is in the first place terribly ingenuous and was probably engendered by a misconceived awe in long-ego canonists of an action that is as accidental (as opposed to essential) as eating and laughing for the human animal. Not only does this misconception entangle church authorities in a web of legalisms such as those already mentioned but, more important, it debases marriage itself. For if the essence of a marriage doesn't exist in the minds and hearts of the parties to it and isn't expressed in their informed pledge to love and respect one another, preferably witnessed by family, friends, and others of the community, it isn't a marriage whether "consummated" or not.

Our developing understanding of the sacraments of Reconciliation and especially of Baptism ought to offer us a model for the development of understanding the sacrament of marriage. (I hope our Catholic tendency to hide our heads in the sand whenever sex is involved isn't the obstacle to such development.) We have learned, for example, that Baptism is essentially the welcoming of a new person, however tiny, into the community of Christians and that pouring water on the person baptized, while an invaluable invocation of grace, is not the essence of the sacrament itself. We have come to realize that there is much more to Baptism than merely the externals of it. The desire of an adult that she or he be baptized (the surrogate godparents when infants are baptized) and the willingness of the community to accept the newcomer is surely of the essence of the sacrament.

Let's hope that we the church will soon file and forget the minimalism that finds the validity of a graceful sacrament in a very mundane act. Christian marriage is surely much more than that.

High-jumping days
are over for Catholics

I hope that American Catholics will never allow themselves to be packaged and delivered on election day by any politician. I am referring to the political ploy that assumes that Catholics as Catholics will meekly ask, "How high?" when a cynical candidate says, "Jump!"

I am a lot more hopeful about this than I was ten or twenty years ago. As a largely immigrant group, Catholics in the first half of this century tended to cling together when any external force seemed to threaten us. And with good reason. Anti-Catholic bigotry was a very real phenomenon here and there was strength in Catholic unity. But while, as Andrew Greeley has pointed out, this kind of bigotry has surely not disappeared, it has diminished considerably and, at least, gone underground. It has become in Father Greeley's words, "an ugly, little secret."

Whether the lessening of anti-Catholic bias is cause or effect, American Catholics have come out of their ghetto in breathtaking fashion since the end of the second World War. Father Greeley, again, has documented the startling progression among American Catholics in both education and income during these years. And for whatever reason Catholics, I believe, have become less and less a voting bloc.

That, of course, does not stop said cynical politicians from feeding pseudo-religious fodder to Catholics (and indeed to other targeted religious groups such as evangelicals) in the hope that they can be milked for votes. So when President Reagan recently promised Catholic educators assembled in Chicago tuition-tax credits for parents of children in parochial schools, no one should have been surprised. I was in fact reminded of Festus Garvey, a political opponent of Frank Skeffington in Edwin O'Connor's classic *The Last Hurrah*. Garvey, when speaking to rallies in overwhelmingly Catholic Boston, rigged a set of ostentatious rosary beads in his pocket so that they would fall noticeably to the ground whenever he extracted his handkerchief.

Not all politicians are cynical, of course, and it's surely possible that one who espouses tuition-tax credits sincerely believes that these are just and good for the nation as a whole. But it is easier to find such sincerity when the President or member of Congress or governor concerned works conscientiously to put such a proposal into effect rather than spitting into the wind, making a grandstand proposal that almost certainly cannot succeed.

I have no way of knowing how sincerely President Lyndon Johnson believed in the substance of the watershed civil-rights law that was passed under his aegis. Johnson was celebrated as an often cynical wheeler and dealer. But, in fact, despite his Southern, segregationist roots, he did much more than applaud civil rights; he did more than any American president, with the possible exception of Lincoln, to make rights for all races a reality. The difference was that Johnson put his "money" where his mouth was.

When I speak of the gradual disappearance of Catholic bloc voting, I am not referring to so-called single-issue voting. Single-issue voting, I think, has had a bad rap. If it means voting for an unqualified candidate simply because he or she votes "right" on a particular issue that the voter feels strongly about, it can be a harmful thing. But if I were black, I would almost certainly vote against an otherwise qualified candidate who was a racist. As a Catholic, I can't imagine voting for an avowedly anti-Catholic candidate whose qualifications in other ways were good. In some such instances, I might have to forego my franchise, abstaining when the choice was between two "evils."

"Pro-life" advocates and voters who strongly favor ratification of the Equal Rights Amendment have an unquestionable right to vote for or against candidates whom they hope will serve their cause. One would hope only that these voters will turn their backs on "our" Tweedledee as decisively as on "their" Tweedledum.

I hope too that Catholics and other religious

Americans will demonstrate that, if ever, they are not now guilty of lockstep voting by spurning another of the sugar plums that is being dangled before them. The proposed amendment to the U.S. Constitution to permit prayer in public-school classrooms would remove a protection that historically has been far more beneficial for Catholics (and Jews) than it has for the Protestant majority. (This is not to say that Protestants should not oppose the amendment just as vigorously. Who will compose the prayers to be said in communities with Catholic majorities?)

The proposed amendment calls for allowing "a nonsectarian" prayer in classrooms but who will be the arbiter of its nonsectarianism? The principal, Mary O'Reilly? The district superintendent, Otis Ellsworth? The Supreme Court?

And in a school where the majority of students are drawn from another culture, what if the prayer would be "nonsectarian" but in a second language? Would the English-speaking minority be excluded as English-speaking students were when prayers in German or French were offered in some 19th-century public schools?

I hope that nothing I say here will be construed as a call for Catholics to "vote their religion." Anything but! I hope rather that Catholics and other religious Americans will strengthen their consciences by bringing the truths of their beliefs to bear upon them and, then, voting their consciences.

Are Protestants better at Catholic action?

Is it my imagination or are members of most Protestant parishes really more active Christians than the members of most Catholic parishes? When I say "more active Christians" I am not comparing the personal religious lives of Catholics and Protestants. I am rather referring to the kind of thing we once called "Catholic action," people acting out their religious beliefs, usually in groups. And these are the kinds of Christian activity that I seem to find more often among Protestants.

Quite obviously some Catholic parishes are beehives of activity and some Protestant parishes are funereal between Sunday services. But more often than not, it seems to me, Protestant parishes seem to have what they call "outreach," groups working for peace and justice, helping the elderly or the handicapped, mission-oriented groups in support of both foreign and domestic missions of the church, and especially youth groups. There must be Protestant parishes without youth groups but I haven't encountered one. In every instance I know of there are young people studying and discussing one area of social concern or another and preparing to volunteer for Christian service of some kind.

I realize that a comparison of Catholic and Protestant parishes is skewed in a number of ways. Catholic parish membership tends to be territorial. All those living within certain boundaries belong to this parish. Protestants, whether Lutherans, Methodists, or Presbyterians, attend, within reasonable geographical limits, the parish of their choice. Catholics have traditionally placed overwhelming importance on attendance at Sunday Mass, to a point perhaps where other parish activities seem de-emphasized. Protestants, on the other hand, may be more inclined to "buy the whole package," to consider belonging to a parish as signing on for a variety of parish responsibilities. Many Catholic parishes have parochial schools; few Protestant parishes do and there may be a tendency to drain resources of personnel and funds into the schools at the expense of other programs.

But I wonder if the difference I perceive between Protestant and Catholic parishes doesn't spring, most significantly, from a kind of arrogance, subconscious undoubtedly, on the part of Catholics. Except in a few musty, right-wing Catholic journals you don't hear much talk about "the one, true church" these days but this concept continues to undergird our outlook to a surprising degree in this year of Our Lord, 1983. It is one thing, of course, to affirm this concept theologically as a tenet of our Catholic faith. It is quite another to project it societally, looking down our noses and thanking God that we are not like the rest of humankind.

We may not be guilty of such arrogance but if we are, our parochial viewpoint could be described in the words sung about that famous beer. To paraphrase: When you've said Catholic, you've said it all. It would be terribly sad if we were indeed saying, "We have the truth right here, wrapped in the napkin of the Mass and the sacraments, and we don't really need anything beyond this."

I have been talking about personal impressions. I make no claim to even quasi-scientific analysis of parochial patterns and I will welcome data from those who have so analyzed or even from those whose own personal impressions confirm or deny my thesis. The last 20 years have been a time of almost continuous ferment in the U.S. Catholic Church and I suspect that these years have been anything but static for most U.S. Protestant Churches and there is much we don't know about the practice of both.

Unless persuaded to the contrary, however, I think there is much truth in my argument. I suspect that Protestant parishes are less likely than Catholic parishes to restrict themselves to teaching Christianity without leading their parishioners in acting out these teachings. The latter are more likely to tell without showing. More likely to say, "Go and act as Jesus did" without helping to program such Christian action.

(It occurs here that I am probably describing mainline Protestant parishes. The more evangelical and fundamental parishes would tend, I think, to emphasis personal salvation with less attention to social outreach.)

But whether I am right or wrong in my analysis, I fervently hope that the kind of social outreach that is inspired by belief in and commitment to a belief in Jesus Christ will flourish and grow in Catholic parishes. I hope that Catholic young people and their parish leaders will invest their talents in programs that have a more Christian orientation than bouncing a basketball or consuming Fritos and Cokes while the band rocks on. (I have nothing against the latter activities. Honest! Some of my best friends do them. So, no angry letters, please.)

I guess I am saying only that being a Catholic ought not to be too little of a good thing. It's too good to be minimized.

Turning back the clock
won't stifle the alarm

We are living, I believe, in the most dangerous of times. The danger I refer to does not come from external sources, although external dangers are real enough, but from within, from ourselves.

The audience for a popular television show reflected the frustrated impatience that we all felt that the former American hostages in Iran had been imprisoned for more than a year by applauding vigorously when a participant said, "I think we should quit fooling around and go in and get them out!" The applauders, apparently, did not question our very ability to "go in and get them out." Neither, apparently, were they willing to face the possibility that some or all of the hostages would have been killed by such an action or that even if the rescue attempt succeeded more lives would have been lost than saved (as was the case in the sad Mayaguez "rescue"). The applauders wanted a simple solution to a complex problem.

Another audience applauds enthusiastically when someone asserts that "the media must be prevented from sticking their noses into things that don't concern them," into the private lives of public people. Once again the longing for the simple solution to an intricate problem is evident.

Whether the procedures followed by our government in its attempt to free the hostages in Iran were the best possible is surely open to discussion. And only a terribly uninformed person would defend the excesses that "the media" are frequently guilty of. But this kind of dissent should not reduce many-faceted, often delicate questions to simplistic right-or-wrong matters.

The problems, I suspect, arise from the fact that our world, our civilization, has become so damned sophisticated that we face and will continue to face problems of sometimes overwhelming complexity. But this situation was clearly inevitable. Our evolution had, as it were, made all the easy choices, only tough ones remain. When our ancestors, for whatever reason, chose to walk upright on only two of their feet, the choice, I feel sure, was simple. But when a little group of scientists underneath the old grandstand at the University of Chicago chose to split atoms, their choice was terribly difficult and some of them agonized over it until their deaths. But if these men were uncertain because they knew that their efforts would make possible lethal weapons of awesome destruction, they realized also that once it became possible to split atoms, atoms would be split. If not at the University of Chicago, at one of a dozen other places.

Today a new breed of scientists, geneticists we call them, can do things that until a few years ago were in the realm only of science fiction. By transferring nuclei from one kind of cell to another, they raise possibilities that sometimes frighten even other scientists. Quite obviously we ask, "What can and should be done about the advances of this new capability? Do we just sit here and wait for an army of mutant monsters to run amok and destroy us?"

If I can't answer that question positively, I can answer it negatively. We can't expect a simple solution to a highly sophisticated problem. There are many shades of gray in the matter and no blacks and whites. There are innumerable nuances that must be examined again and again as a jeweler examines a diamond under a high-powered glass. Moral and probably legal questions must be raised and an enlightened attempt to regulate genetic experiments must be made. But anyone who thinks it is possible to stop genetic experimentation entirely is a fool. Mountain climbers seek the top of Mount Everest "because it's there." So, do scientists seek the next step after this one. This is the way we are made and that is the way our evolution leads us.

We all have nostalgia for the way we were, for a life that in recollection seems to have been simpler. This nostalgia ebbs and flows but it seems to be especially strong today. (It may even have had political effect recently.) We see it in many places. In religion, it takes the form of trying to wish away the theologians who continue to explore and to raise questions they consider unanswerable. "Honda makes it simple," the dulcet offscreen voice of Burgess Meredith tells us. That may work for the auto manufacturers but it's not true to life.

As much as we might like, we can't turn back the clock. And the danger in trying to do so is that we might fall victim to authoritarianism, to "a man on a white horse," or more likely to a totalitarian bureaucracy that will restore order through simplicity, that will sing the siren song offering us the late-20th-century equivalent of "making the trains run on time."

God forbid that we will settle for this in our society, in our government, in our church.

Protests should stay out of harm's way

On the evening news not long ago we watched a group of local suburbanites demonstrate against the opening of a Planned Parenthood office in their neighborhood. The demonstration was anything but massive but it was not insignificant. The protestors made up in intensity for what they may have lacked in articulation of their grievances.

I comment on this particular demonstration because in many ways it was a model of the kind of street theater that has become so much a part of life in the United States. It was sharply focused, nonviolent, and the protestors were people directly affected by the object of their protest. The number involved was in proportion to the gravity of the problem and except for a young, teenage girl who was clearly hysterical when interviewed by the television reporter, the demonstrators were reasonably restrained.

Not every viewer, of course, (or for that matter, every neighbor) would agree that the opening of a Planned Parenthood office was an unmitigated evil but the protestors were merely exercising a right guaranteed to Americans by their Constitution and sanctioned, now more than ever, by successful enactment.

Can anyone believe that the gains in civil rights effected since 1950 could have been achieved without the demonstrations in Selma, on the Washington Mall, and in countless other parts of the country? Would the war in Indochina have finally been halted as it was without the nationwide demonstrations that telegraphed to government officials the widespread opposition of Americans to the war? And there is general agreement that the quiet demonstration by perhaps a million Americans in New York this spring opposing nuclear armament gave pause to even the most hawkish political leaders.

Not everyone admires (as I do) the courage and persistence of citizens like the Berrigan brothers who devise and take part in a seemingly endless series of maneuvers to publicly reprimand the pursuit of nuclear war aims. Their courage merits admiration, I believe, because they are always willing to take the consequences of their actions. Most have spent time in penitentiaries and all, by the openness of their actions, seem willing to pay whatever price our society deems fitting. Their persistence, I think, is even more remarkable because they surely realize that constant repetition of their acts of protest will, inevitably, yield diminishing returns.

But despite the good that demonstrations and acts of protest including picket lines can accomplish, they are open to abuses. Anyone who witnessed via television the heroism of Martin Luther King and those who followed him can not have forgotten the heartbreaking spectacle of protestors being humiliated and physically abused without striking back in any way. King was a disciple of Mahatma Gandhi who brought the mighty British Empire to its knees by his willingness to protest nonviolently. But nonviolence seems particularly difficult for Americans. Maybe it's our frontier tradition. Maybe it's the cockiness that comes from "punching King George in the snoot," from "Don't tread on me!" from being King of the Hill so long. We see this strain where union pickets start out peacefully but yield to rage and strike out at nonstriking "scabs" crossing their lines. And that, I think, makes all the difference.

To be just, demonstrations and protests must be nonviolent. They must do no harm intentionally to other persons, whether adversaries or bystanders. If they do damage to the property of others, the protestors must be willing to indemnify the property owners, either monetarily or by their labors. (I doubt that the original saboteurs made restitution for the machines their wooden shoes destroyed but if they did not, their actions would seem not to have been justified.) And protests should not infringe the rights of others. It would seem legitimate for protestors to bar access to, say, a nuclear weapons plant, temporarily and briefly, to symbolize the protest. But I cannot see any justification for an attempt to bar access permanently.

There is an assumption here that we are dealing with a democratic society in which individual and societal rights are respected. In a totalitarian society, the kinds of protests proscribed here may be a last and only resort.

Making distinctions can be tedious and they may try our patience but they are essential in a society that cares at all about morality.

Holy Chief, we praise thy name

This is not a political essay. It is, in fact, an anti-political essay in the sense that it concerns the abuse of politics. I make this point at the outset because what I intend to say requires me to mention the names of political figures but, it should be noted, I am not judging them but rather some of the people they encounter in their public lives.

Viewers of the evening news recently were treated to the spectacle of President Reagan addressing the national convention of the Knights of Columbus. Predictably, the President told his audience what he was pretty sure they wanted to hear. He denounced abortion, praised prayer in public schools and tuition tax credits for students in private schools. Only his criticism of a nuclear freeze was at all controversial and, given his audience, was not likely to arouse a chorus of boos.

I say that the pattern of the President's speech was predictable because telling audiences what they want to hear is the nature of the political animal, Democrats and Republicans alike. (The only exception that comes to mind is Adlai Stevenson attacking military buildup before the American Legion convention in 1956 and we know what happened to *his* political career.)

My objection in this instance is not to what

the President said but that he was there at all. I do not believe that religious groups have any business inviting public office holders of any political party to address them substantively (excepting, that is, "welcome to our city" speeches). I object to this practice philosophically because it violates at least the spirit of church and state separation. I object to it theologically because such practices blur the distinction between theistic and civil religion. And I object to it practically because it can easily compromise the integrity of the religious group by advancing the cause of a politician who may later embarrass it. (A picture comes to mind: Several of the most prominent members of the Roman Catholic hierarchy beaming their approval of Richard Nixon during his 1972 presidential campaign when unbeknown to them, Nixon was already up to his hips in the Watergate immorality.)

Let me back up and set the scene I saw at this year's Knights of Columbus convention. Ranked up behind the lectern at which the President spoke were rows of bishops dressed in episcopal cassocks and crowned with roseate skull caps. This garb, appropriate for purely religious functions or within the confines of Catholic parishes or institutions, seemed glaringly inappropriate at a function that became so clearly civic when the President gave his strikingly political speech. In the Catholic ghetto of Rome prelates so dressed are sometimes seen on the streets and in other secular places but in the United States where the grace of freedom from religious persecution has showered so many blessings on Catholics, it would seem that even our body language should salute the separation of church and state.

If the President had been merely a nonspeaking guest at the Knights of Columbus convention (although even that gesture might have been unwise), the standing ovation he received on his arrival could be justified as a token of respect for his office. But what of the standing and prolonged ovation he received at the conclusion of his talk? Didn't that link an organization so staunchly Catholic in its ideals and goals and so clearly identified as Catholic in the public eye with a leader clearly representative of a particular political party and, beyond, a particular political philosophy? Have we learned nothing from the tragic coupling of (Catholic) church and state in so many European and Latin American countries?

In one final footnote on the Knights of Columbus convention, it was difficult for at least one viewer not to sympathize with the plight of Cardinal Casaroli, the distinguished Papal Secretary of State, trapped as he was on the podium with no choice but to clap along with the others as if he were helping to welcome the guests on the Johnny Carson Show.

Politicians, in the United States at least, would seem to be wiser or perhaps less naive than churchmen. When Protestant Richard Nixon opposed Catholic John Kennedy in the 1960 presidential race, the former looked for every opportunity to appear before and speak to Catholic groups while the latter did the same with regard to Protestant groups. That's the way politics is played and I see no reason to blame either Nixon or Kennedy for acting as they did. It was the religious groups that were foolish enough to let themselves be used.

There are, it seems to me, more than enough men and women of stature and wisdom, not actively engaged in politics, who are available to speak to every religious meeting of any kind. I hope that all religious groups will avail themselves of such well-qualified people and resist the temptations of seeming flattery.

Isn't "Holy God, We Praise Thy Name" just as spirit-raising as and much more appropriate than "Hail to the Chief"?